Things I Found .

N J Campbell

For Shaun, Israel and Silas.

My love is with you. Always.

Thank you to Lucy, my editor.

Forever grateful for my diamond among the magpies.

In Sarajevo
in the spring of 1992,
everything is possible:

you go stand in a bread line
and end up in an emergency room
with your leg amputated.

Afterwards, you still maintain
that you were very lucky.

Izet Sarajlić

It was a few weeks after the bad thing happened, a few weeks after the news and the telling of the news, that my mother called.

'*I have been thinking you know*' she says with a soft pause '*I have been thinking that I had you when I was 37. In the 1970s, that made me an old mother.*'

'*It's not old now*' I say. '*It's a really normal age to have a child.*'

'*Yes, I suppose. But I was just wondering if the egg was old. Maybe everything is my fault, because the egg was old.*'

Another pause.

'*What I mean is, I think maybe you are just a bad egg.*'

She stops, then repeats, sounding sorry.

'*Just a bad egg*'.

Chapter 1

The beginning

There has to be a beginning.

My beginning is just the scene-setting, the drawing of a neutral background to start a story that came later.

Or my beginning is the roots of everything, roots which tangled into my bones. The stories that come later were the inevitable consequences of the starting gun.

It doesn't really matter.

But this is how it happened.

I was born on a sunny Friday in June 1978 in the West Midlands. The sun was in Cancer. Gemini was rising at 3.30am as my mother pushed me into humanity, whilst my father touchingly ate a tomato sandwich and read the *New Scientist*.

My father stayed blurry in the background. He taught science. He sat in his home study behind a typewriter and was very over-protective of sellotape and other stationery supplies. The sounds of his 80s work-shoe heels coming home was an edge. My mother cleaned buildings in the village, my brother and I came along and ran wild on polished floors. I played Bingo with pensioners at the Lunch club, and ate coffee cake at the Nearly New shop in the community centre.

We listened to *Slow Hand* and *Mouldy Old Dough*. My mother sang *Groovy Kind of Love* in the kitchen.

My parents fought loudly, viciously, endlessly. Sundays collapsed into themselves. There were delicious roast dinners and puddings with jam and custard, and then a walk in the grey and green of the forest. But then waves of tension, like white lights, could not go out. Our cassette players taped the best of the

Top 40, but it could not save the day. Curtains were drawn as soon as light fell, and then there was darkness between rooms and between us.

Primary school smelt of bleach. Kerry and Wayne tipped over the sand tray and were locked in the Wendy house by Mrs Fell. A small toy sat on your desk when it was your birthday. Margaret Thatcher took away our break time milk.

I became convinced on a regular basis that I was eating someone else's packed lunch. The horror of eating someone else's sandwich would not go. I worried about germs, unnamed sickness and dirty hands. My mother agreed and warned me about sausage rolls and cream cakes.

My brother read ferociously, book after book, after book. The Library Van visited the village once a month, and we could climb aboard to choose. When the reading stopped, we taped our voices, scripted little plays, made music and wrote stories on scrap paper. We pretended to be the Brontes. But he could not always play, his head hurt, his eyes were often half-closed. His first word as a baby had been *Gone,* an early sign of his inner romantic, melancholic reaching. His childhood was a headache.

My first word was *More.*
More, More, More.
This is as an inner and obsessive need for *things to always be happening.* My antidote to it was to touch items in sets of threes. If you don't say the number loudly enough, you would have to start again. Aside from compulsions, I focused the rest of my mind on being cosy. I liked to pretend my bedroom was a cottage, where I took in homeless guests – or more specifically abandoned babies. At night time though, my bedroom cottage lost its warmth and became a place full of ghosts, ghost children. The only thing that would keep them away was trying to imagine *Nothing.* The time before the world, when there was *Absolutely Nothing. Nothing* would bring me fleeting joy, but then my brain would demand I return to earth and it was gone. I was back with the ghost babies.

I would then have to resort to humming songs we sang daily at school; the 1980s children's classic *Make Me A Channel of*

Your Peace, two songs devoted purely to the eradication of litter: *Milk Bottle Tops and Paper Bags* and *What shall we do today to keep the playground tidy?,* and a song well chosen for very young children, that we enjoyed while the head teacher played his guitar, the traditional Irish lament, '*Whiskey in the Jar*' – the tale of a robbing highwayman who is betrayed by his woman and becomes an alcoholic.

We ran on sugar because it was the time before anybody had started measuring it. Our whole bodies were made of Ribena and Angel Delight and Penguins and Artic Roll and French Fancies and Orange-flavoured clubs, but we could run it out across the bleak fields at the back of our house. We were let out. We went on bike rides alone. We could hide amongst corn where a frog once sat on my naked foot. We collected ladybirds in a lunch box to keep in our dens. Kate Bush sang in our heads. We went home to watch the A-Team.

On summer evenings, the garden smelt of creosote drying on the shed. If ever there was a danger of lightening, we pulled out every plug in the house as a matter of immediate urgency. We all enjoyed power cuts, which came in frequent spells.

My father ate noisily without joy or hesitation, and I once felt compelled to put a fork through his nose. I wasn't punished which suggests he felt I was somehow justified.

We visited many churches and lit candles. We went on endless camping holidays; rain on the tent, the shipping forecast on the little radio, a bag containing soap and toothbrushes you took in turns to the wash block. I sat on a fishing stool and wrote in a diary with a lock. Our parents argued when the lights went off. The rain never stopped. A thunderstorm was a treat. The greatest treat of all; a fire spreading from fields to our campsite. We shouted '*Have you lost your dog?!*' across fields to a man, I presume we thought had lost a dog.

We watched a man drown on the beach.

I cried during all birthday parties, including my own. I couldn't explain why. My adult self would say I felt a kind of existential sadness about time passing. Or maybe I just didn't win all the games. I wanted to win, but I also wanted to be an outsider. My hair was uncontrollable curls. I couldn't be one of the ponytail girls.

I once woke in the dark of night to find my room flooded with strange light. I thought it was an angel. Sometimes I still think it was an angel. Mostly I think I had a temperature.

I tripped into the dining room wall through a hula hoop. Blood circling my mother's turquoise dungarees, as my parents raged about if I should go to hospital. A firework set fire to my holiday shorts. An Alsatian bit through my thigh. I fell down every stair of the staircase, into a foetal heap at the bottom. I went head-over-handlebars on a fast bike, with cuts layers-deep surfacing everywhere. A cricket ball hit my temple. There was hallucinating food poisoning after my father fed us raw farm milk in the heat of a French holiday. We pretended to smoke with pencils on our Tomahawk bicycles. My brother's pencil slipped and cut into his throat. A friend threw garden secateurs at his head. A bee stung inside his mouth, which apparently gives you the gift of persuasion.

There are few photographs, but silent cine film recorded by my father. We had regular home viewings, the projector piled high on books. We always seemed to be running my brother and I; towards the Cornish sea, then away from the sea, then to the end of the garden, and then back again, right up to the red light of the camera.

The children from the children's home across the road visited us and my mother taught them to make scones. I showed them proudly the compost heap in our garden and we picked mint.

We visited regularly my grandmother's large and disintegrating Birmingham Georgian house. I was soothed by a wooden box that contained tiny farm animals. There was regular talk of ghosts, which meant I couldn't go upstairs to the loo alone. It was here once, as I washed my hands, my mother said triumphantly *'Fancy me having children!'*

Later, my grandmother lived with us for a year, and did enormous amounts of ironing and passive aggressive television scheduling. She told me the complete story of *Jane Eyre* whilst I lay on the sofa with a fever, page by page. I gave her recorder lessons, which I charged at 50p per hour. She taught me about justice and community and poems, and injected pacifism into my blood. Her favourite two stories were: how she broke up a fight between two men, one of whom had an iron bar, and how she bought a homeless man a sandwich from Marks & Spencer, but he rejected it because he didn't like cheese.

We visited my other grandparents in Devon. There was fried bacon for breakfast. The wardrobes were full of potent home brewed beer. My Nan pushed a small trolley from room to room, which held an asthma inhaler and Reader's Digest. My brother devoured the back issues. I watched ITV, which in their house was loud, constant and in extreme high contrast colour, and ate pickled onions.

Birds banged into the windows of our house. My mother nursed a cuckoo back to health.

We attended Hands Across Great Britain in 1987 – a national protest against unemployment. There weren't enough hands in our village to link with the next village, so it was more Hands Across A Small Section of A Village Road. My brother had the horror of holding hands with his school teacher. We helped our father put Labour leaflets through local doors.

Birthdays and Christmases were rich and magical with surprise, organised by my mother, with love. There was a doll and a Care Bear and a Globug and Speak and Spell. My father made me write to Margaret Thatcher to ask her why most of our toys were made in China or Hong Kong, and no longer the UK. Later, we had a Spectrum 128k. We were the generation who could wait patiently for 15 minutes for a game to load. It seemed a small price to pay when you were witnessing technological miracles.

We spent the night in the car parked in a Welsh quarry.
We slept in a trailer tent on the hard shoulder of a motorway.

We wore cagoules with alarming frequency. I had a disproportionate understanding of how often this word was in common usage.

There were endless picnics. We sat on our camping groundsheet on a Welsh hillside or in a Derbyshire field. I have never felt so hungry. Afterwards, my father would walk several metres ahead of us. If he joined us, it was to show us a bird through the binoculars.

We went to the local town for the first time when I was 9. Nobody has a clear re-collection as to why almost a decade passed without us leaving our village boundaries.

I also spent my first night away from home aged 9. There was a school trip to an outdoors activity centre. I remember my pride at having a reversible tracksuit to wear, my tears at losing a ladybird shaped ring, and my joy at our *squad* winning the most *squad points.* I had been a key player in the number of points – I had earnt us 10 for being the only girl who would touch a worm.

There were three cats. One was flattened in the road as a kitten.

My father bought a canoe. My brother and I were disappointing canoeists. It didn't help that we were learning to canoe on a little scrap of murky water near a large grass wasteland. My brother's athletic best friend was more enthusiastic, although he briefly capsized into the dark brown depths. The journeys home from canoe days seemed to be dusky; we were winter canoeists perhaps, or my memory is clouding over my sense of failure into half-light. On the capsize day, the air was heavy with blame. I remember lying stretched out on the orange sofa watching *The Karen Carpenter Story,* crying tears for Karen and for canoes.

We watched, among a crowd, as a huge barn in the village burnt to the ground. Our clothes at home were deliciously smoky.

Not far from we lived, a new cul-de-sac was built with homes that looked like large dolls houses. My mother and I made frequent visits to the show home, which had gold taps, wall to wall pine, draped curtains in peach, Laura Ashley bedspreads, and a clear glass dining room table. For me, it was an impossible bubble of glamour and luxury, a little glimpse into a world of imagined perfection.

Secondary school smelt of chewing gum burning inside porta cabin radiators. You could survive by painting Tipex thinner inside your cardigan to inhale during Maths. Someone fell to the floor turning blue. Someone else was told by the Career Advisor they should be a Shepherd. Our French teacher cried through an entire lesson. We were her breakdown. Boys spat in the corridors.

There was a school trip to a *Country Show*. We all bought pretend cigarettes from the gift shop which contained white powder that we could puff into smoke. We were surprised on the coach that one boy had also bought a hamster.

There was a swimming party where the birthday girl got her first period in her white swimming costume. My bleeding started on Christmas Day. At school, if we had to miss communal showers, PE teachers recorded our menstrual cycles in a notebook. They also checked our feet each term for verrucas. We were ashamed of our bodies in quiet compliance.

At home we were latch-key kids, who ate multiple fun-size Mars-Bars and said mean things to each other. I spent hours alone in my bedroom, where I enjoyed putting a screwdriver inside a switched-on blow heater in an attempt for fire. Later, I watched soap operas on my black and white TV. My father would occasionally open my bedroom door and shout '*EMOTIONS!*' and then close the door. This one man campaign against having feelings would not prove effective.

I lived for *Smash Hits*. When my magazine came disappointedly with a Brother Beyond badge, my mother tore a badge from another issue featuring my beloved Jason Donovan. This was technically shoplifting, but for me it was an act of true courage and heroism.

We watched the Berlin Wall come down.
We sang for Nelson Mandela.
Freddie Mercury died and my brother switched from white sports socks to black ones in mourning and has never looked back.

I passed from reluctant piano lessons and a love for Jason and Kylie, into cigarettes and new breasts. I discovered Prince. I cried tears for Kurt Cobain. I enjoyed my green eyes, and introduced them to eyeliner. I watched *My-So Called life.* I decided to skip low self-esteem, and went straight to empowerment.

My mother talked to me a lot about beauty, and her own unique opinions on sexual currency. I had babysitting jobs each week, one of which was for a couple in their 60s who needed help with their grandchildren. One evening, the grandfather gave me a lift home in his sports car. *'It's your birthday soon?'* he enquired, as we swept through the country lanes. *'Yes, I'm 16 in a few weeks'* I replied. *'There is a big difference between 15 and 16'* he said with a knowing pause. *'You know that don't you?'* I nodded yes, as his hand gently squeezed my thigh. We arrived home, and I went straight inside to tell my mother. *'Well'* she said *'I have always thought, he is a very attractive man.'*

Meanwhile, Zammo and the Grange Hill gang had told us to *Just Say No,* but we became the generation who *Always Said Yes.* There was weed to smoke in bedrooms out of windows, at parties in parks, at gigs where nobody cared, and in boyfriends' cars in the middle of the night. There was LSD and magic mushrooms, there was watching time stop. There was very short skirts and jelly-shoe heels and fake fur coats. There was amphetamines and Ecstasy. Lots of Ecstasy. There was waiting to come up as you followed the Rave signs along the country lanes, or as you stood shivering in the queue outside the club, fake ID burning in your pocket, hoping you had timed everything right to fit the music. There was hard house and techno. There was underage sex, and then better age-appropriate sex with the boys you really wanted, who knew what to do. There was missing school for drugs and sex. And there was the arrogance of knowing you were clever enough to fill in the blanks.

There was the handsome boy from the biscuit factory who was embarrassed by his estate and the dogs being fed in the bathroom. He loved me. He gave me water when I took the pills, he drove me home, he protected against pregnancy like a disease. He was very respectful of other people's sofas when he visited me at the babysitting jobs. He taught me how to find dealers you could trust. He made me mix-tapes. He was devoutly sexy and strong and handlcd the police during two car searches like a lawyer. But I had Running Away in my eyes.

There were exams.

There was a holiday with friends in the Canary Islands and a beautiful boy from Switzerland.

There were the girls who got pregnant. The boys who became heroin addicts. The girls and boys who would never leave your village, your town, and your judgement for them. As escape became all that mattered.

I filled in the university forms without help or context. I picked Politics as a course without information, like a name from a hat. I picked the city of Leeds with careful consideration, based on club flyers and a new interest in drum and bass. I wrote on my accommodation form '*Please do not put me next to quiet people*'.

There was a dis-used railway line next to our village, closed by Beeching in the 1960s, isolating fields and farms from towns and cities. We ambled here as children and skinned-up as teenagers, jumping from fastener to sleeper, skimming gravel across the abandoned platform. We were told that sometimes a goods train would pass through.

What would we do if it did? Would we dive into ditches? Would we cling to the rusty staircase that led to nowhere? Would we be flattened like cartoon rabbits?

Later, I looked up when the last train passed through. It was 1984 - when I was six.

Twelve years of thrill and worry, looking over your shoulder backwards across the tracks, all for nothing.

But now, I was leaving. A new line to a city.

I had suitcases and CDs and posters.

From my parents, I had black humour, the comfort of darkness, the knowledge of no happy endings, and the freedom of emotional detachment.

I had family stories of Judaism, Spiritualists, Ghosts, Angels, Baptists, Pacifists, Socialists and Trade Unionists.

The neural pathways in my brain were formed. The psychological foundations were built.

I'm out. Free.

9

Gone.

I'm a university student in Leeds in the late 90s. Britpop is riding high; I'm musically Blur, but socio-economically Oasis, so I sit on the fence with Elastica and Suede, until we all find Jarvis Cocker. My uniform is flared jeans or corduroy, converse trainers – as a nod to Grunge which we have sadly left behind in our small towns - and a lot of eye make-up. I'm surprised by my new flatmates and the baggage we have all dragged to the door. Two of my new friends have left public schools in the South; I have never heard of gap years or Kettle Chips, never used 'hectic' as an adjective or had days that were 'nightmares'. I have never been told I can succeed. I am expected to succeed. I must succeed.

I'm surprised by ambition, virgins and people who go to lectures. I have zero expectations, no interest in work and full commitment to hedonism. 20% of me is a disjointed fraction of a self I once was, 80% is solid re-invention as I shop for an identity. Re-invention is the joy and gift of the young and responsibility free – but of course, we flush our freedom down the toilet and do all the other cliché things to waste youth that we were told we would.

I pick courses that contain boys I fancy, which gets me into trouble when I sign up to Theories of Politics in Russia, which I cannot follow or fathom. The boy is tall and Bowie-esque with glamorous scarred cheeks, but the sacrifice of my thing with him is to run from the class when it is my turn to answer questions and hide in toilets. I'm not even ashamed to do this. Sadly, the internet is still just a dream around the corner, so there are few opportunities to shortcut or plagiarise, which in hindsight saved my skin, because I would have cheated if I could.

There is much talk about New Labour. We are as high as kites when Tony Blair heads to Number 10, and get higher still on Ecstasy at a club night, where Michael Portillo's face of defeat as he loses his seat is shown on a dizzy loop.

My friend B and I give ourselves a self-conscious label of neurotic; which means a free pass to attention seek, chain smoke, not get dressed and occasionally throw things out of windows.

We also have synchronised morning-after pills and vomit into our sinks.

A boy in the flat below shoots another boy through the thigh with an air-rifle. Nobody thinks this is particularly disturbing. We accept all circumstances because we are new friends, because we are children, because we are self-medicated and because we are wankers.

I take too much speed at Jungle nights, and ketamine by mistake. I don't sleep for days and bore everyone with my endless comedowns. The Kate in my head changes to Nick Drake.

I am briefly obsessed with a skater boy with a very beautiful face who introduces me to the smoke of heroin, and after sex tells very long, humourless stories about travelling. He leaves a trail of things wherever he goes; a lighter, a piece of his trousers, coins, wraps of foil, receipts. Unfunny and hyper-messy are two major deal breakers, and it is all over very quickly.

My friends and I brew potent mushroom tea. I venture out to a world of only shapes and colours. Back at our flat, my flatmate has set up a horror show, with words of fury on the wall in tinsel and blades arranged upright on the table. We are ridiculous, we are failing, we are sliding. Either we never had common sense, or it has been temporarily suspended in a parallel universe full of adults.

I am 19 in Dublin. I'm an angry drunk.

There is also a trip to Amsterdam, which of course, boringly, I cannot really remember.

I get a part-time job as a waitress in an Italian restaurant, where I accept without question the dress code which is *very short skirt*. I get £3 an hour, large amounts of garlic bread, some very large tips and quite a bit of free cocaine.

I fall in love with the most beautiful of boys with cold blue eyes. Our energies are mismatched; I'm a terrible misjudged firework, he is some kind of tropical sea, still and warm. He is the lead singer and guitarist in a band. He has a beautiful voice;

11

we have the same kind of pretensions in our brains, and a need for endless romance.

A group of us get a brief summer job on a mushroom farm. We pluck mushrooms that look like little snowballs, sprouting from soily beds inside a dark shed. Pat, the supervisor, ensures we are keeping up our picking output. One of our friends gets 'picker-of-the-day'. We emerge, blinking at clocking out, too selfish to realise we are just tourists amongst real workers who work inside the mushroom darkness for years.

We move from halls to a disintegrating house, 8 of us, 1 in an undecorated basement, proudly boasting of our proximity to England's most burgled street. Blue Eyes and I are now housemates, and a couple too, an intense beginning. We have separate rooms, mine in the attic, but drag mattresses between our spaces at ungodly hours of the night, or balance our sleep in a single bed.

We argue. A mattress falls down a long flight of stairs. A lamp is thrown against a wall. He drinks to oblivion and wakes in the night to pee over his guitar.

My housemate A and I take it in turns to go to our local corner shop, which we affectionately name the Dog Shop, due to its intense smell of Dog, despite the fact we don't actually ever see a Dog. The Dog Shop sell single cigarettes at the universal rate of 20p each. This is a dying trade, an innocent time that we don't want to let go of. A sometimes buys his dinner from the Dog Shop to eat on a tray, which we find both hilarious and depressing.

There is a group trip to Edinburgh in the summer. We sleep in a hostel where a woman in one of the bunks is a permanent resident. We wake early, hungover, in half-light to see her pulling on her post-office uniform and packing her few possessions into a plastic bread tray. We make enthusiastic friends with Australian tourists and later regret our friendliness when they track our scribbled addresses and turn up to stay.

There is another trip to the South of France. We have heard you can pick lemons (or was it melons?) so we travel without purpose, without maps, without planning. There is a lot of cheese and tomatoes, and a lot of wine. Blue Eyes and I are having a lot of sex in a tent, which must have been annoying for everyone else. We never make it to lemons or melons, after camping out on a traffic island and having our possessions stolen. We make it back to Nice by hiding inside the luggage section of a train, next to bicycles. We are marooned at Nice Airport for 36 hours, with a few wet wipes, an incomplete set of passports and dwindling cigarette supplies. We are dirty, tired and stupid.

Our house is burgled. A small child pushed through a tiny window by an adult to grab anything – a little bit of cash, other things I cannot remember. I am haunted by the idea of the child trained to steal, but these thoughts are taken over by Princess Diana. The morning radio tells us she has died; a car, a tunnel.

People start to send emails and talk about websites.
Somebody has a mobile phone.

The band has many gigs. I write some lyrics, but really I'm just the girl with the band, with the main boy. He sings along to Smashing Pumpkins in the shower. He is childlike but charismatic. He doesn't speak till about 3pm and then stays up all night. I talk and talk and talk, and there is a lot of silence.

His father lives in Hong Kong. He goes to visit. I write him notes to open, one for each hour of the flight. He comes home with just one in his pocket – on which I wrote *'Being away from you feels like I am wearing only one shoe.'* This nod to incompleteness at his absence, was both unpoetically described and untrue. I'm not sure we did miss each other. We believed wholeheartedly in the concept of obsessively missing someone. We had signed some kind of contract of emotional dependency that it took many years to break. I guess that is where the shoe comes in – you can't walk down the street, you can't live, you aren't free. You've got one fucking shoe. And a wet sock.

We travel to Prague and take extraordinary photographs, mainly of ourselves. We have an argument on the plane, which culminates with him having a nose bleed. I am not proud of this moment, but we are now defined by drama and it would be a sort of betrayal to try and be normal.

His mother in London is hospitalised with an episode of deep depression, there have been many before. We go together to see

13

her on the train. Her empty flat has a cake iced with '*Let's Celebrate!*' on the kitchen table, and sad books, books that would tell us her story – turned away with their titles hidden from us on the shelves.

The second year of university ends with some pot-washing in Bradford, making some sandwiches for solicitors who were not impressed with the daily dozen potential filling options, and a stint at Butlin's for Blue Eyes and I. For two weeks, we live in the caravan, sleeping in a plastic bedroom. We get up at 6am to dress, shivering, in our uniforms, and walk slowly to the holiday restaurant. We wait tables at opposite ends of the large room. I'm in the premier section. We carry multiple stacks of plates and worry about getting shut in the freezer rooms. A pot-washer smashes pots across the wall when he gets tired of washing them. After our evening shift, we drink and argue. On our last night, we smash our caravan window – the cost we must pay to have it fixed is most of what we have earnt. There is silence on the train back to Leeds.

My friend K has gone to Vancouver, Canada for the summer with a work visa. I decide to follow; there is no part of me that wants to go, but I drive myself to organise it. I feel I should do something for myself. Blue Eyes and I say goodbye, with huge theatre. We believe this to be an expression of great love, but of course it is something else, and it is something that makes you feel unwell. I leave in the middle of the night on a coach bound for the airport, and spread myself across two seats. It is impossible to sleep because the driver has to tell us when we are in Derby or Milton Keynes, so there is a lot of waking with sick jolts. I eventually make it to Heathrow, and my lonely morning flight.

I'm on a trip that I am only physically complicit with.

People on the plane are watching *Titanic* which seems an odd choice.

As I slip on my courtesy socks and eat my packet of nuts, I'm starting to become emboldened by solitude.

But the clouds I'm sitting on are silent. They are only there to carry us.

My next round of jolted sleep against an air-plane window is innocent.

And then, there it is - my first Canadian light.
Was there sunshine or darkness? I don't remember.
What was happening at home, in the village? Did a parliament of magpies flock on the fields, as if in conversation? Or was there just a grey sky that had forgotten me?
Who knew, who could tell me what was coming?
It will be an ill-fated trip. There will be pain – waves of pain – and the waves are on their way, ready to break over me, and wash all that went before away.

The plane comes in to land. The wheels, the noise, the abrupt halt.

Chapter 2

When Everything Hurts

I'm 20 years old, and I'm in Vancouver, Canada for the summer. I had not read anything about this city until I land in it – and although it is beautiful and the people are extraordinarily nice – it is not my kind of city. People seem to love roller blading. They trail through Stanley Park in lines, only moving aside to let the joggers past. I have never seen so much sportswear. The people I am sharing my hostel room with talk enthusiastically about saving enough money to ski in the North of the city.

I like a filthy city. I like grime. I like excess. I'm not ready for sports. The blossoming, endless sunshine and goodwill makes me feel as if I have emerged from under a stone.

I am mentally saved by the chance meeting of two new friends, Irish boys who have also almost certainly emerged from under stones. We rent an apartment together, which contains only a table and a few chairs and blow-up mattresses to sleep on. M is the grown-up of the arrangement. He is patient and wise beyond his years, has already secured himself a brilliant summer job, and is there to keep the rest of us on the right side of something. S has a brilliant mind, the most brilliant I have encountered. He sits hunched over books, stewing in information, while his bagels burn in the kitchen. He drinks cup after cup of tea, sweating but committed to his ritual. Their warmth and intelligence is infectious and comforting and addictive. I want to talk to them forever. We play *Closing Time* by *Tom Waits* every night. I forget who I used to be.

There are hazy evenings; I remember an older, rich man who pays for my night out, there is some angry drinking and idiotic sign stealing, and there are nightly chats alongside the sea. My friend K is working in an unapologetic hippy shop, with patchouli and crystals and clothes in every colour. We meet a man called Dolphin. I get a job in a dollar-pizza store. I give you your pizza slice. You pay your dollar. It's late at night, so you might comment on my breasts or just chat to me, or maybe swear in my face. Then I will sweep the street outside and walk home hungry with a very small roll of notes in my pocket.

There are six weeks of this summer. It passes quickly. Blue Eyes sends me a love letter, and I miss him, although I read the letter only once. One day in the park, a French man presents me with a poem he has written for me, before disappearing without a word. This act of extreme romance energises me for days and I re-read my poem to myself, and anyone else who would like to hear it multiple times.

One evening, a group of us watch the UK's entry in the *International Festival of Fireworks* on the beach. I am enthralled, and take photographs which will never come out. One is taken of me, hair tied back, large smile. It becomes one of those accidental shots; a picture that will assume a significance that does not yet exist. The innocent flash, the press of a button, before the future rolls over it. My friend S is busy writing anagrams in the sand. My full name is shuffled to spell *A Sharp Humid Joint.* We kick over the grains. We don't yet know my name contains the future.

The next day I am unwell. Just a headache at first, a few Tylenol needed. And then a raging, raging fever, one that brings dreams and terrible thoughts, as I try to rest on a deflated mattress. Then there are stomach pains that double over my body, and diarrhoea which never stops, and is full of blood. A few days later – and I am feeling stronger. The germs must have passed. I celebrate with some orange juice. And then in the middle of the night, as I try to sleep now on the floor with just a sleeping bag, two toes on my left foot start to throb, a pulsating pain. A pain that will not rest. By morning, I cannot walk at all on my foot. When I look in the mirror, my eyes are completely red and horribly sore. I sit with S; I remember I am wearing just a bra, a towel wrapped around my bottom half and flip flops. I have a black hat covered in glitter. He is making me tea. I am trying to smoke an ill-advised cigarette. I start to cry, and in my tears are blood. I'm actually weeping red like a statue of Jesus. S is jubilant at this moment of tortured, religious glamour, and we laugh heartily at this sudden and strange new talent. Then we go to the Canadian ER.

17

It costs me $195 dollars to be diagnosed with an eye infection and a foot infection. I am given antibiotics.

I cannot work in the pizza shop and I am running out of money, so mainly I sit in the park. I can walk only a short distance. I am listening to *Ladies and Gentleman We Are Floating in Space by Spiritualized* and nothing else.

I wake into another painful night; the toes across my right foot have now joined the symphony of pain. I can only shuffle along, holding onto walls and people.

My parents arrive in Vancouver. This was a planned holiday where they were supposed to arrive to find me having a wonderful time, and then they could enjoy their own adventure that I have talked them into. They are irritated by my shuffling state. My father throws away my new Acupuncture trainers. He has decided they must contain some kind of vicious bacteria. Now my bent toes poke out of sandals. It is not a good look.

My parents return me to the ER. Another wad of dollars, after which I am informed I do not have any kind of infection. I am given very strong painkillers. They take only the very top of the pain away, like cream from full fat milk. I cannot sleep.

The pain has spread to every joint in my hands; I grasp at make-up brushes and see glasses slip and smash from my hand. I return again to the ER. This time I receive a gown to wear, lie in a bed, and have my blood collected. There is a lady having an asthma attack and vomiting between breaths, and a man who wants everyone to know he has pain in his testicles. I pee in the bottles and have all the X-rays. I am asked about sexual health and recreational drug use in front of my parents, which for a few minutes turns the pain into numbness by the horror of exposure.

I am diagnosed with a type of reactive, inflammatory arthritis, for which I am given anti-inflammatory medicine. My parents disappear to North Vancouver. I have spent $800 dollars on medical bills.

The pain continues, it never stops or lessens, it comes in hot waves like acute embarrassment. Time takes on a new kind of dimension, things appear in layers. My ankles start to swell, now I can hardly fit my feet into any kind of shoe. My shoulders and neck start to creak.

I take my fourth trip to the ER. I feel out of my own body by now, just an object with mechanical failure. I talk to Blue Eyes on the phone; all I hear is a tiny voice, calling out sympathies, lost across a sea. I am given stronger painkillers. This medicine too does nothing; just sugar pills – but I haven't yet learnt anything about becoming a placebo.

I take the ferry to Vancouver Island with K and my parents. There are endless skies around our tiny, pretty bed and breakfast, owned by Darleen & Russ. They pick us up after dinner in their truck. Their home is wall-to-wall white carpets, we tiptoe barefoot on snow drifts.

Back in the city, the pain has spread to my knees. One is swollen, too large for jeans to pull over it. My parents schedule me a flight, and take me to the airport. They tell me that I let myself get run down, I didn't eat or sleep right, my adventures were unplanned and impulsive, and this is what happens. *This is what happens.* They remain on their holiday.

I'm on the plane alone. I have a fever, and this one is angry. I'm sweating. But my lips are so cold, they are blue. I'm watching a film, but I don't understand who anybody is. Where am I going? Where did that city and its new friends go? All is dissolving. Those roller blade lines. Those joggers. Those burning bagels. That mattress that lost its air. These joints and bones that have cracked and creaked on a naked floor. The dollar slices. Who will cut the pizzas now? Who will serve in the middle of the night? Who will be called a fucking whore? It seems important. I need to know where I belong in this summer, I need to know what remains.

I'm a child, but now I must nurse myself and I must grow up. I must ask for a wheelchair as London arrives, because I am falling down and away, and I am sick, so sick. I am wheeled out to Blue Eyes' mother, she has come to collect me in a taxi that she cannot afford, and cries tears for me. I lie in a delicious bed in her flat, welcoming English sleep. Blue Eyes arrives. He looks happy like a beautiful mountain. I panic at reunion, and start to brush my teeth with antiseptic cream by mistake.

Nobody really talks. I am propped up in the back of Blue Eyes' brother's car and driven to Leeds. The tide of pain continues to rise, walls of fire. Leeds looks reassuringly small and grim, like a dirty factory. At the student house, I weigh myself and find out I am 7 and a half stone; a whole stone and a half, 21 pounds, 9.5 kg has been lost like luggage. There is so little weight on my hips they now click dangerously as I walk. My cheekbones are outrageous. I must not enjoy them because they are a sign of ill-health, but of course I do. I am a woman, I have been raised in heroin chic. I have finally achieved it.

I sleep, sweating. I dream about a rubbish heap of thin bones, bones that dislocate, bones that click like teeth, crack like nuts, bones that are used as knives. Joints that have burnt away, leaving singed holes on the heap. I live on this heap, obviously. I do not know what country it is in.

I am admitted to hospital.

I have my own room, I briefly fantasise I am a private cosmetic surgery patient. But pain doesn't let you daydream for long. I can only lie on the bed. I can only watch television programmes that mix into my temperature, with plots I can no longer follow. I don't know who anybody in *Neighbours* is any more. *Home and Away* seems complex and intelligent. Cilla Black has a new show called *Moment of Truth* where children are visibly distressed as their family lose large amounts of promised prizes which have been wheeled out to them. On *This Morning* they are doing a live test of Viagra. I switch off the screen. I turn instead to read my mounting Get Well cards. One of them is completely blank but comes with a toy monkey who looks very sad.

The Doctors inform me I have a very serious case of reactive arthritis; the inflammation has spread from joint to joint. Nothing can move or work until my immune system can be placated like a furious dog. I am an interesting and rare case. Students surround my bed, they have come to take photographs of my fleshy limbs. I realise many are the same age as me, which makes me want to evaporate. They are shiny and achieving, while I am motionless, unclean and stuck. I don't want to be rare. Just normal.

Blood is taken daily. There are more bottles of wee and a cardboard hat to shit in. Occasionally, I crawl from my bed to my private toilet where I lock the door and cry. I'm now full of all

20

the drugs; temazepam eyes, dihydrocodeine fingers, steroid cheeks, morphine, morphine – a regal queen with its own pump. But the pain remains. Blue Eyes brings me lilies, the flowers of death.

I watch the world from my bed. I'm in a rheumatology unit – where most patients are elderly. Wheelchairs slide past, there are tip-taps of zimmer frames. I don't talk to anyone. The nurses come when I bleep, and I bleep all night. They tell me to cheer up, but frown at my temperature which won't go down, and my blood pressure which mounts and falls, and my arms and legs which are fat and misshapen and useless. I cannot eat. The smell of the dinner trolley turns my stomach. And everything comes with gravy, so much Yorkshire gravy. And custard. Floating puddings in thin custard.

I'm given an 'awake' operation on one knee, which I watch on the screen in horrified fascination. I see the gold injections slide into the sinews.

My fever ends. I become strangely cheerful and am moved to a ward where I meet my new ward mates. Opposite me is Susan. We talk about our knees. There is also Nellie, a grandma, who is making rapid progress through a stack of Mills & Boon, which she calls her '*filthy books*'. Hilda is an elderly spinster. She says '*They are long days, aren't they?*' several times a day – in between short trots to the toilet. She is a baby pony, her buckle-shoes clip-clop, clip-clop. She lives in a care home. She tells me that sadly she doesn't have any friends there, because she won't play Bingo. I want to hug and squeeze her and soothe her, or maybe suggest the merits of joining in games, but I also hate her when I hear the clip-clop, clip-clop. I am ashamed of my irritation.

Janet spent last Christmas in Florida. At night, when lights go out, she puts on her sleep tape. We all have to lie in our beds and hear the tape. Every night. The others start to doze very quickly. I'm awake and raging. The fucking pan flutes. The fucking wind chimes. And the final climax – water racing and dropping? Surely not a waterfall. Now very much awake, I need the toilet, which it takes me 20 minutes to get to. Alan, the only male nurse, bangs on the door and asks me if I need a laxative. What I need Alan, is a fucking shotgun.

There are no guns here. No exits. No alarms, and no surprises, just like the song.

Blue Eyes visits every day. He is at a peak of handsome heroism and everybody wants to fuck him. I am told constantly *How Lucky I Am.* He is of course, not lucky, just lumbered with me. Sometimes he helps me have a bath in the disabled bathroom, and I wash my hair until I almost flood the floor. When we leave the bathroom together, two nurses stare and giggle. Do they really think we were having sex in a medical toilet? Do they really think we felt desire as we saw the swinging disabled hoist where old ladies sit naked every day? Old ladies who are lowered into tepid water, by hungover nurses, who feel sickened by old loose flesh? I am ashamed of my contempt, but it keeps on boiling, boiling inside.

I have injections into all of my joints. They forget the local anaesthetic when it comes to my toes. *'Sorry, Sorry, Sorry'* they say. I say *'It's fine!'* But I will remember the feeling of that needle sliding against my bone for the rest of my life.

Susan is replaced by Edith. Janet leaves with her tape. Edith is smug; *'I am a 79 year old miracle!'* she exclaims *'I have a pacemaker! I survived a car crash! I have a glass eye!'* She talks about me to her visitors in a whisper which is the volume of normal conversation. *'Look at her!'* she points *'Only young, and she walks worse than me. And she is anorexic too. Doesn't eat a thing!'*

I draw my curtain and say *Cunt* very loudly. In case anybody has missed the first one, I repeat it. *CUNT.* I close my eyes, and find I don't have anything left to cry about.

I am sent for a bone scan. This is in a separate building to my ward, so I am taken in a wheelchair by a very beautiful porter to the little bone place, and I am all excited about fancying people and also being out of the ward on an outing. The scan is conducted by a very short man with glasses, who I do not fancy, but he seems very kind. Chatting away, asking me a million questions, rubbing the scanner over my body. At the end of the scan, there is a moment of quiet while he busies himself with looking at data on his computer, the silence is weighted, a little odd. I realise that he is also now rubbing the scanner between his legs, over his erection. He is making a little sighing noise. *Am*

22

I imagining that? Is he making that noise? I feel nothing. The beautiful porter comes to collect me. I want to tell him; *is that the right thing to do?* The trouble is I feel more normal than I have felt in a long time, and I am not upset. I tell nobody.

Pat and Ann have joined the ward. They call me 'sweet pea' and buy me Kit Kats. Pat vomits all night, a tsunami of dark brown sick which reaches my bed in pools. It's a horror film. Ann gets up to help *'What's all this brown stuff?'* she keeps repeating. *Its vomit Ann. It's fucking vomit.* The emergency doctor is called – apparently she is vomiting shit – her bowel has become blocked. I get dressed and shuffle out to the reception area, find a seat and put my head against the wall. A nurse asks me if I would like a cup of tea and a biscuit, which I politely decline. She is eating a sandwich on her break. I'm surprised she feels Pat vomiting shit is a good moment for snacks. I mean I won't eat for at least 24 hours after I have witnessed poor old Pat vomiting shit.

Sylvia arrives. She likes to point at her catheter bags *'Nurse! Change this*!' A pause. And again.

I talk to Jean, who wants to tell me about her divorce. *'I felt like a caged animal'* she says, *'And now here I am caged in my body'.*

I think a lot about if I am caged. It seems a problem which I must work out. I can just about hold a pen now, and sit late at night to scribble in a notebook. I write out a series of slightly deranged questions to ask myself.

Am I caged in my body?

How do I feel? Am I angry? What am I angry about?

What am I supposed to do?

I scribble answers. I think about answers. I don't ask anyone else about answers.

I realise that I feel caged, yes, trapped in pain. Physical pain is relative; it doesn't matter what the ache is, it cannot be graded. Doctors will ask you to score your pain out of 10. There will be people with a paper cut who will say 10, and women in childbirth who will say 0. There are stoics, and people just too polite to complain, there are martyrs, and yes, there are people who make a fuss. I realise that my old body no longer exists, it ended with the firework photograph. The toes that first found the pain are

23

now bent and will never straighten. All the joints in my right hand will quickly become fused, so it will never bend fully again. I will have to adapt to its strange shape, my alien hand. There will never be another day when there is not joint pain somewhere in my body. I cannot exist in a world where I am waiting for pain to stop, because that is no longer a possibility.

I understand the cage is all mine, I am building a story around my body and I have to stop.

I think about being angry. I'm angry that this has happened. I write it down in lines and lines, like a detention schedule. The more I read it, the more of a child I realise I am. What did I expect my life to be? Did I think nothing would ever happen to me? Or that only things I had imagined or controlled? Did I feel entitled to happiness? Or at least an easy life? I had thought I was empathetic, that I had acknowledged the suffering of the world, even if I had not felt it. I thought I knew my own privilege, but here I was making it the star of the show. I was self-important. But I could forgive myself.

Life is problems.
Life is problems.
Life is problems.
Life involves pain.
Life involves pain.
Life involves pain.

And so, there it is, my body is me. My life is my life. This is the first thing I feel I have ever learnt. Being angry with my body, is to be angry at myself. To be angry at this situation, is to be angry with my life. All of life. The plan. The chaos. The unfairness. The randomness. The joy. The pain.

And so I have to embrace my swelling joints like strange new friends. I'm going to befriend pain, I'm going to never forget my position on the relative scale.

I'm in hospital for a long time. I get much better. Home is very strange at first. The bathroom doesn't smell of disinfectant, nobody is going to hand me a menu card to choose my order. I can sleep at night, the fluorescent lights have gone out. I don't have anyone to bleep. It is hopefully going to be a while before I smell vomit.

And when I wake up in the morning, I feel joy, actual joy, at the ability to walk. The chance to hold a mug of tea. Shoes that fit on feet. These are now pleasures. My final year of university has started, and I need to catch up. Yet my new information about my body, and about pain and life, do not appear to be transferable skills. I'm kinder now, I'm happier, I'm stronger – but there is no way to convey this to the people around me. My friends sail past in lines, unware of chance or change. I don't want more drugs or raves. I'm studying. I have a new found interest in Radical Political Philosophy. Habermas and Foucault are my new companions.

I push myself too far and get a strange post-viral exhaustion, which is like a descending fog that means you cannot stand up, and that 12 hours sleep is not good enough. I return home to my village.

I force myself to take a tiny walk each day; the church, the pond, the train tracks. I try to read.

My mother nurses me with love. She buys me a second-hand black fur coat which makes me look like a gothic red-riding hood and definitely represents my inner autumnal gloom, as my life sits on hold. I fill time, and fill days and fill up a shoe box with little thoughts written on scraps. There is a family trip to a Brine Baths – where warm salt waters are supposed to soothe your bones. Blue Eyes comes too. He tells me later that my father had a hot soapy shower in the changing rooms, so he saw his penis. I find this funnier than is necessary which is a good sign for recovery.

I'm also now bored. I don't know when you draw the line and state you are well. My parents are arguing in their perfectly timed repetition, its familiarity is a deadly hum, a ticking clock. The best thing to do is just stay still. Don't move during the clatter of kitchen implements or the shuffle of slippers; stay frozen till it passes. I keep going to bed; handing each bad day to the past, who takes them greedily and absorbs them into the back of good days, which must be on their way.

We take a pre-Christmas trip to Devon, and my brother who was previously living in his car, but now has a new Northern life, comes along. In an act of odd generosity and misunderstanding of taste, my father buys us tickets to *Cinderella on Ice*. To further aid regression, my brother and I sleep on camp beds in my Nan's house, and have an argument about the ownership of sleeping bags.

In January, I return to university. I'm still isolated by my body, by difference and change, and I worry when I can't sleep. The illuminated clock shines in my eyes and seems to spell Arthritis. My mother sends me a parcel; Marks & Spencer vouchers, chocolate and a note which says: *Eat well, Sleep well, Work Hard, Be Nice to Everybody.*
I'm not sure I am doing any of these things.
I write notes to myself. *Do what you have to do. Be on your own. Get things done. See what is missing. Try not to make plans. Sleep. Ignore the pain of your bones.*
My brother and I visit Nick Drake's grave on a rainy Sunday. *The movement in your brain. That sends you out into the rain.*
I do some limping and some laughing.
I call myself names in the bath, because my body has changed. I imagine myself to be a kind of insect. My hair smells of wool. My head is ticking over illness.
Good days come.
Whole years pass with only background pain, soft murmurs. Then pain and swelling returns in phases, knees that forget to bend again. A jaw that locks.
I go to see a new rheumatologist, he places firm hands on my swollen ankle. And then quickly, like a dart, he fires off *'Any more lumps or bumps?'* and puts his hand on my breast. He moves it so fast, in swift arrogance, his own denial. I can't be sure he did it. He has got me. I can only walk out. I don't feel any other powers are available.
In a few years, there will be the sudden loss of ability to walk in the weeks before my wedding, and there will be two operations. One will remove a rare benign tumour from my knee; it is so special the NHS have to find me a very specific surgeon and pay for me to stay in a private hospital. I will wake from the surgery to find out I am shaking violently and being given sedatives. The pain will be way more extreme than I imagined, and the cut to take it out will require 30 staples. I will carelessly lose 2 pints of blood. I will sit all night with my old friend the morphine pump again, and feel a bit worried about the fact I seem

to have had this surgery on the night of a full moon, and I will have an oxygen mask and a few fairly unpleasant hallucinations. I will convince them to send me home too early, and will spend six weeks barely able to limp. I will have purple bruises across my leg that are actual hand prints. The wrestling of a surgeon, while I slept under the ether.

There will be pain. More pain. Sudden jolts of raw agony will shift me back in time to the germs, and the reaction and the disease and the lost summer. But my knowledge, learnt across the sea, will make me disassociated from the trivial and the mundane for always. This is a gift.

And so, each time the pain waves come, I will remember that the pain is me. That I am my body, I am not separate to it, and I have to love its failings and its agonies.

It is not always easy to do. There is a lot of holding your own hand. A lot of deep breathing and imagining pain as some kind of warm source of water. There is a lot of standing and staring at your feet, and remembering you stand in your own space, and that might be all there is. Just standing in space, perhaps hovering on some sort of existential map of problems and pain, as you remember again that you were never entitled to anything different, nobody is. I am entitled to what I give myself; and what shall I give? Jokes. Dance moves. Songs. Words. Kindness, kindness. Thoughts of Nothing.

So I close my eyes and imagine the people you can only imagine; the other people in pain, the many people in pain. People covering up pain, discarding pain, and overcoming pain.

The overcoming is in the ownership.
Write it down.
Life is meant to hurt. And that's OK.
Write it down.
Hold the waves. Hold again. Keep holding.
It will be OK.
This is an order. This is a promise.
This is sometimes all you have.

Hold.

27

Chapter 3

Losing It

In those odd days of recovery, as I put my bones back together, and re-joined my life, there was a new feeling. It began as just a faint sense of unease; an odd foreboding, occasionally a brief and cold sweat of impending doom.

At first, it was easy to solve. I had to stay in touch with sets of threes. My touching had to be secret and quiet, or you started again. My innate tidiness was now a sort of inner threat; my room must be immaculate and ordered – or trashed, things broken, everything on the floor. Middle ground was disappearing into a sinkhole.

I returned to university as everyone else moved towards graduation. There was relief and sadness. I was ready to say goodbye to sitting on plastic chairs in kitchens, smoking through the same conversations. I didn't really belong to the night, and its drugs and music anymore. We all stay in a camping barn, somewhere in the Yorkshire moors, and I'm really angry. I cannot control how things are ordered or arranged here. This is a new revelation and one I must immediately anaesthetise with huge amounts of alcohol and bottle smashing and all-out unhinged unforgiveable idiocy.

The summer has returned.

There are more feelings, or are they just thoughts? Death mostly. Death around the corner. Death at my doorstep. Rising to Death. Sinking to Death. And religion. Talking to a God. Not Believing in a God. Worrying about God. My new and greatest fear; eternal life. The horror of always existing.

The thoughts are becoming harder to quieten. At first, I can wash some dishes or write an essay or have a shower, and switch them off. They grow arms. Now they want to talk to you when you are brushing your teeth, when you are lying down to sleep.

They grow legs. Now they want to remind you as soon as you wake up, that they are still there. These thoughts. These thoughts. And you cannot make them go.

Blue Eyes and I plan a trip, with rucksacks and tents. We fly to Italy. Pretend we are famous in the airport. Look fabulous. Have our luggage lost by the airline. Chain-smoke. I'm ravaged by food-poisoning-paranoia so eat only bread, cheese and chocolate for a month. At night, I have new feelings, the doom has risen to a detached sense of claustrophobia, as if you are wholly trapped in your own personality.

There are nights in hotels and also very cheap campsites. Bologna, Florence, Venice, Verona. Blue Eyes playing the guitar to willing audiences, despite the smell of shit. Large amounts of arguing and sex. One argument combines the two and I write about it in my diary; *He used up all the hot water repeat-washing his penis. What a selfish cunt.* He is not writing a diary, but if he was he would say; *She is turning into an angst-ridden bitch'.* I'm not sleeping, and it's not just because the tent is sweaty and lying on stones. My mind is racing, racing, racing.

We take the train to Austria; Salzburg first. The total solar eclipse of 1999 darkens our carriage, but we are unmoved. We are not looking at the sky enough, we are more focused on the slowness of the train, and lederhosen. There are real lederhosen, and they appear to be everywhere in a way that is more fascinating than any kind of pink moon.

We take a hostel room. Blue Eyes invites an American guy who has nowhere to stay to sleep in our room. This would seem a terrible idea on any level of reality, but in my current mind-set, I am about to be raped, tortured and murdered in my sleep. I set hourly alarms on my watch to check that this stranger, at the foot of our bed, is still soundly asleep. In the morning, I vomit out of pure distilled anxiety and do not speak to Blue Eyes for the next three days. In silence, we visit Hallstatt, a tiny village in the mountains, take a cable car to explore an ice cave, which is not romantic, just cold - so cold, and then there is Vienna. We negotiate it without any communication whatsoever. I confirm that Ultravox was right and that Vienna *Means Nothing To Me.* I break the silence with this joke, but nobody is laughing.

We book into a hotel where paintings are haphazard on the walls, and I'm not sure the sheets are clean. I strip them all from the bed. I feel the rising doom and the anger, and drink a very large amount of cheap gin, which was quite possibly paint stripper. We walk along a confused foreign road to a bar, where I immediately fall unconscious. Blue Eyes carries me home with physical strength fuelled by rage. It is the most drunk I have ever been. He does not forgive me.

Our final stop is Hungary. The guards on the train, with their guns, tell us we have to pay supplements to get off the train. A man from Chile who I have been flirting with for the entire journey while Blue Eyes sleeps against the window, pays them for us.

We make new American friends in Budapest. We visit a dirty bar, where there is much cocaine in the toilets, and gambling at the tables. Our new friends are filmmakers and film our night. It's mainly me talking to the camera, grabbing distraction and attention where I can.

Our bags are lost again on the way home. I leave my passport on a National Express coach.

When September arrives, Blue Eyes stays in London and I return to Leeds to finish my course. My friend K and I are renting an attic flat. We have a tiny kitchen, a tiny bathroom and a room each. Her room contains a sofa to operate as a lounge, while mine contains a table and chairs to be our dining room. There are strange handprints all over the loft hatch, which are quite scary when you get back from seeing *Blair Witch Project,* although in retrospect, the most terrifying thing is that we re-light our boiler which repeatedly stops with matches.

I'm trying to study. I'm trying to keep the creeping darkness at bay.

I travel to London to see Blue Eyes. I'm on a tube in rush hour, which gets stuck in a tunnel. At first, I look at everyone else; I see nonchalance, calm, irritation. We are stuck a bit longer. And then it comes. My heart starts to bang, bang, bang against my chest. I'm trying to suck in breath from the space, but the space is too small. And we are stuck, stuck, stuck. My legs

30

feel thin and paralysed. I try to practice all I have learnt and apply to my aches, my body aches, but it doesn't work. This is my mind.

We move. The doors open. I race out, up the steps, onto the street. I sit down on the pavement, gasping, gasping. Terror is pushing hairs on my arms into upright arrest, its forcing open my eyes that cannot take in the enormity of the sky. My internal organs are arrested and frightened and fucked. I don't move for a long time. I don't know about panic attacks or anxiety. I don't know anything.

No, I do. I do know. I'm fucked now. This new agony I cannot survive.

On the train back to Leeds after my visit, I am completely motionless and frozen with claustrophobic fear. I move not once. Not to pick up my phone or a book. I wet my pants because if I stand to find the toilet I will remember I am trapped and out of control on a tin-can train. I knew this would happen, so I am wearing three pairs of pants and a pair of tights.

In Leeds, K repeats answers in the attic and makes tea. But I'm in bed now. I'm in bed. I'm here. Only here. Books cannot be read. Music sounds different. Food is a horror show. My digestive system has resigned. My adrenalin is having a house party.

I don't know what this is. I don't know what this is. But I'm done, I'm done.

Sleep is the only refuge, but is hard to find.

I have to get out of the bed. I've already lost too much time to a bed.

So I learn to split my mind; there are my actions and my words – these are beginning to seem more reasonable and measured. I'm following a routine. My thoughts and feelings are terrible secrets; just fear, and darkness. They run as a simultaneous internal dialogue, while I fake-laugh, drink with friends and do exams.

So I'm an actress.
I'm a brilliant actress.
I'm a functioning human being.

31

The new century arrives. The bug doesn't bite. I'm in a field in Suffolk making people chant *The Millennium Prayer* which is all about having a new start. My mother tells me that people are buying into spiritualism, but missing out Jesus.

Yes, I think I am.

I get a good degree, but feel nothing. I graduate mid-year alongside nobody else and there is no ceremony.

I need to earn money, so I'm editing foreign language translations of instructions to computer games in somebody's conservatory. I'm doing fundraising for a museum, where you get a free lunch in the café. Somebody vomits up their tomato soup over their table because it has a hair in it, which will never leave my top-five most dramatic responses to a not-really-very-bad scenario.

K has spells away from the flat to begin her television career in London. She replaces herself with J who only eats crumpets.

I work in a bank for a week. My job is to turn pages in folders, removing slips of green paper. There are 100 pages in every folder. There are 100 folders. I do this for 7 hours a day. Nobody speaks to me. I work at a builder's yard, where I type letters, take phone calls and have to laugh at jokes about blow-jobs.

I work in the office of a Trade Union. I make a lot of tea, and accidentally tip over a very large shelf of books and pot plants for which I am made to feel as if I have committed murder.

I'm still acting.

I'm still functioning. The thoughts, the feelings remain. Resolute. Touching sequenced objects is the only slight relief I feel.

I make the only decision somebody can ever make when they are anxious, depressed and possibly on the spectrum of Obsessive Compulsive Disorder. I decide to move to New York with Blue Eyes, with very little money, where I will work in a job I have obtained over the internet, as a carer for adults with learning disabilities. What could possibly go wrong? What other possible options could there be?

I leave Leeds. I pack some bags. I find it very hard to talk or eat. I don't remember the airport or the journey. I still have my ticket from the flight on which I have written on the back in red lipstick *Keep breathing. Everyone thinks you are normal.*

And so we go. And so we arrive, we arrive in something else. We take a bus, and then there is a cab through our new city. Film scenes run behind the glass, just hyper-reality, just neighbourhoods crashing and falling. I remember Times Square lit up in the darkness – of course I do – but I also remember arriving at the hostel in warm incessant sunshine. Memories deleted and blurred by the effort of survival.

The hostel is on the Upper West Side of Manhattan. We are living in separate dormitories. Travellers swarm among us with their endless chat, and we try to filter out people who wish to live in this city like us, to make friends. We meet a British music promotor who gives us tickets to see David Bowie play an intimate gig for about 50 people. I'm so close I can smell his beautiful Bowie skin. I meet a Muslim girl from East London who has run away from her very strict family to visit her white American boyfriend she has met online. He is dying from leukaemia. Except he isn't. And he doesn't exist. And now she is stranded. We meet a once accomplished actor, now down on his luck, bankrupt at the hostel – waiting for a pay check from *Sex and the City* to get back his apartment. We visit our friend made in Budapest whose boyfriend is a fashion photographer. By week 2, Blue Eyes has a modelling contract with an international agency.

As my boyfriend begins a new life, rushing on the subway to castings and go-sees, with his 'book' full of new beautiful shots, and as he builds a new band, starts new gigs, sings new songs in different venues, I begin my job.

On Day 1, I'm taking a group of developmentally disabled adults to New Jersey Shore for a week-long vacation with two other leaders. We negotiate 4th of July traffic in our mini-bus, to a coastal resort called appropriately *Ship's Bottom.* I'm definitely at the bottom of something, and there are also many bottoms to clean and dress. I have to learn fast – in my group I am caring for a blind woman, a low-functioning elderly woman who can barely walk and a woman with Downs Syndrome and Alzheimer's. We must manage a budget and medications. We must entertain with food in diners, the zoo and the frenzied casinos of Atlantic City.

There is also a three-hour whale-watching boat trip. When I return to New York, I'm deleted, depleted, dark.

In the City, I slide into Blue Eyes' life. We have new famous friends, with silly cars and endless party invites. We have nights out in Brooklyn, with flowing coke and immaculate people who seem to have been cut out of magazines.

The next trip is to New England. There is Rhode Island – where there really is absolutely nothing to do whatsoever, and then there is Boston. There is an aquarium and a seaport and a jazz festival. A lighthouse. A member of my group has an ear infection, so I have a nostalgic trip to the ER. There is a deaf lady with few words, I teach her new and important ones: Vanilla Ice Cream.

And then there is Lisa. I remember wheeling her plastic suitcase into the motel. She has goose bumps on her thin, crooked legs which hang out of a tennis skirt. At the Chinese buffet, she is making a little moaning sound. The group want me to do something, and I'm doing my best to hold her.

We don't get there.

At the motel, I stand her naked in the shower, facing the tiles, and she is crying softly as I wash the diarrhoea from her legs. I throw away the tennis skirt and her yellow underwear in a blue plastic bag. She sits in bed in her clean pyjamas and tells me she loves me.

10 days later and we're back in New York. I carry my responsibilities and bags down Amsterdam Avenue, wearing $7 silver sandals which are cutting into my feet. I have a hostel bunk bed; I'm woken every half-an-hour when someone puts on the light, and get my towel stolen from the end of the bed. I spend most of my time in the East Village, buying shoes and seeing bands. I can't use the subway now though, I feel too closed in. And elevators are also avoided. I know avoidance is the food of all of my monsters, but courage is wearing thin. It takes all of my energy to stay with the performance.

On a bright Thursday, we drive to Pennsylvania. The group are excited, there is a pretzel factory, and a place where they make those little chocolate kisses. We are staying on an Amish farm, where the puritanical commitment to lack of technology

34

seems quite selective. It is OK apparently, for the Amish to have their own movie theatre, but this only shows one Amish film. It is a light story about how if you enjoy yourself, you will go to hell. I'm glad the IQ of most in our group means they cannot hope to fathom the message. For many of them, hell has already happened. There was a baby that had to be given up. There is a brutal lobotomy scar. There is a black man covered in the cigarette burns of his racist carers. But I'm here, and I'm resolute, and I'm high on *making a difference,* and making sure the sedatives are issued on time.

On the last morning of the trip, I'm changing the colostomy bag for Gloria, and I'm asking myself softly, and quite reasonably, how did I get here? I'm holding a bag of someone else's poo, while puritans in 17th century dress walk in lines pass my window to pick corn on the cob.

What is this? Who am I now? The only thing I do know, is I must not stop. If I do, the darkness begins to creep, the thoughts, the reality inside. I might forget how to act. I might falter and slip from the stage.

And where to next?

A summer festival for hundreds of disabled people. A real festival with wrist bands and mud, branded t-shirts. It's a closed world. I breathe through mounting panic. I try to do a good job. I breathe. I'm still breathing.

And then to the Bahamas – a trip with higher-functioning participants. A trip where Ernest from Harlem sees the ocean for the first time, where one participant proposes to another (who accepts) and I forge a friendship with my co-worker A. We sit and chat by our tropical sea, take a tiny bus around the island, and eat in restaurants which are just islanders' front rooms where you eat what they happen to have cooked in the kitchen.

There is a Caribbean cruise too, a meandering ship dropping us at islands for short stops, where we only clock-watch and make sure we don't lose people, and buy terrible souvenirs, before we return to cabins. Cabins that slide at angles due to a recent hurricane, and leave us mopping sick from every surface. At midnight, the American ship rings its bell for the All-you-can-eat Midnight Feast Buffet, and we sprint to catch our group members at their doors, and steer them back to bed, in a war against over-eating and more sick mopping.

I take another group to a special summer camp. I sleep in a wooden cabin and have a complicated schedule of medications to give my participants. I successfully perform the Heimlich manoeuvre on morbidly obese Anthony, who is chocking on a piece of steak. I break up a physical fight over a girl who won't wear knickers. I enjoy Michael who says a hundred times a day, and almost in response to every question '*Well, I'm black*'.

Next is Vermont. We are driving on Labour Day, and we are navigating poorly, in the time when you only had paper maps. There are no services on the highway so we stop at a Dunkin' Donuts. Two participants have had accidents, and we trail them, and their unapologetic leaking bodily fluids through the kitchen, with the donut makers looking on, to the tiny staff toilet. We don't even buy any Donuts. It takes us 10 hours to reach our motel, arriving at 3.30am. Our group in the van are in a foreign hour, silent and blinking in the darkness. The next day we go to Ben & Jerry's Ice Cream World, and then take a boat ride. Vermont is beautiful, a defying expanse of breath-taking green, huge rolling hills that go on for miles.

And then I'm back in the city, and I must carry on. I must stay in character.

I speak to my mother. I'm carrying my new knowledge of the real world like a gun. I want to give it up, lay it down, so she can dismiss all my fear away, like she could with old fear, when it was just swimming lessons or fireworks. But I can't. This is how people get lost. When something seems so terrible, it can never be confessed. All the words in the world are not enough.

We have moved out of the hostel and are now renting our own room in an SRO (Single Room Occupancy) in an apartment building on West 94th street. Blue Eyes and I cannot afford the full rent, so are sharing the room with a Brazilian couple. We sit in the airless room, with its stifling heat, opening and shutting the one window that works. We have two flat mattresses on the floor and two unrelated chairs. One is blue in office design, the other green and bohemian. The Victorian mantelpiece holds an assortment of books and odd things, flowers in a pot. We have a sink, a cooker and a fridge. There is a dirty bathroom on each floor to share with our building housemates and the occasional rat. The four levels of stairs elevate through levels of smell; cheese and spices cooking, juices of fermented rubbish, babies' nappies and disinfectant. This is where we may be able to love each other, the love of a connection and a plan. We listen not to our words, but Spanish phrases at the door, a phone in the hall, a boiling saucepan.

My first fall arrives, and in upstate New York, it comes in nine different shades of red. Our group are high-functioning, and we can leave them to wander the dude ranch. We ride horses through the forest, take a hayride through the hills, eat cream pie in the cowboy barn. At night, I sit with my co-worker and new friend A, smoking out the window of the wooden hut. I can stay a little while here. I'm not missing bagels in paper bags, obscure films, acoustic open-mic nights. I don't want to go back and count dollars from a shoe box, or turn pages of *Complete Chinese Medicine*, looking for the page with the answer on it.

I keep on.

I keep on.

But now, fear is moving into new hours, not just late night or early morning tremors, but ordinary time fear, which means you can't finish your lunch. I'm aboard a tiny, tiny aircraft, drifting to Nashville airport. We are staying in a Southern hotel, overlooking a cargo rail track that shakes the windows. A member of our group is paranoid and over-medicated. Another is insistent at bedtime each night, to ask me when Liberace died. After the Grand Ole Opry, we finally reach Memphis. I can't believe how dusty Graceland is. My group cannot stop giggling, a spreading hysteria, even graveside as we add flowers to the endless mountain for Elvis.

After this trip, I'm glad to be back at the apartment, I smell of emergency. Our Brazilian friends have left for California Dreams, so now the apartment belongs to us. Blue Eyes is waiting for me in the middle of the room. We have a party to go to; I am a purple dress, gold shoes, pink fur cardigan, black eyeliner, velvet lips. I boil frankfurters in a broken pan. At the party, I pass toilet paper to Lil' Kim and say all the right words.

But I come home early on my own, and he doesn't come home at all. I sit and wait at the window, drinking cold tea. I'm waiting for the moment he will be returned from the dead, the key in the door, the look on his face, will bring everything home. Time betrays me, and brings light and breakfast. I eat iced coffee buns and finally go to sleep. I get up to walk in circles around the block, past the bus-stop where a sign says *You Live in the Most Exciting City in the World. So now what?*

I'm off to Philadelphia. We are celebrating a birthday with cake, but our participant is very worried it's the wrong time for cake, and asks me to check the time. He must also ring my motel room hourly throughout the night, to both announce and check the time. I understand the checking I really do. When the phone rings each time, I wonder if it is my brain calling. We get lost on the way home, and I sit in the front seat eating the remains of a vanilla circle, studying the map. Medications have to be done in the bus, with a bottle of flat soda and quite a few pills dropped under the grey seats.

Next is a flight, perfect and horrific, to Orlando, Florida. It was only a matter of time. The group are in two rented condos, white bungalows on a white road. I'm in *Edward Scissorhands.* We have a man called Albo, who smells of mould. He is lifted into the bath, washed with lime foam soap, but still smells of mould. We take it in turns to change an elderly man who wears diapers. Another needs scrubbing clean in a public toilet, needs changing into Hawaiian shorts. He can't stop grinning. At Disneyworld, I stand in line for a long time to see the man in a suit. Mickey appears just as I am administering benzatropine. Later I share a cigarette with Steve at sunset, trying to cut through his naïve danger, with trails of godly light. I hold onto a flirtatious wink from our diaper man, who, devoid of senses, has just a little sexuality left. And, then there is someone else, on another birthday, sniffling over a cake, as they cheer for memories. This is important to them, so it will be to me. Love is on all corners; even in the first November I have ever seen such sunshine, even on Disney streets where I am a European rock.

Blue Eyes and I don't know what to do for Thanksgiving. It is cold and windy, and I'm wearing a fur hood and $1 gloves. We sit at our round table and eat perogies and potato salad. I draw astrology charts in bed, hunting for stars. The participants call me to tell me about their kittens, and obsessions with drinking water or collecting watches. At night I feel the black uncertainty of my new life. It is like looking down from the rooftops, measuring the space of a jump, trying to imagine what it might be like to shake your brain, fall through your own head, to a stop.

But this fear thing, it is still here, a Red Ghost. It becomes harder to stop. And I've been sent back to Orlando, and all its kingdoms, to look for more magic and animals, to wait for the parade. I'm holding the panic in, rushing through the days, counting the moments back to New York, shaking on the plane, wanting for it all to be over. Back here, with him, the Red Ghost loses its edge, becomes a matted ball of electric hair positioned in the centre of my chest. I focus on the Christmas lights, ignoring snowflakes falling on Manhattan, which only trap me further on the wrong side of the map. I feel the gap of the ocean, smiling, turning in the dark, arms outstretched. I lie in bed, my feet on the floor, and know I am trying to live for a God that I am glad isn't real. But, through the sheet at the window, I can only see a street lamp and an empty, foreign sky, somebody else's horizon. The city won't let me go.

My mother might understand. She tells me on the other end of the pay phone that I should mentally draw brackets in red ink around bad thoughts in my head. I love her, but am now living behind glass, on the other side of the sea. A man with one hand sells me an egg sandwich, tobacco and hopeful looks.

We fly home for Christmas. I'm not sure how it happens. I count every half an hour of the flight with new terrors, until the lights of London. It is a winter Thursday, and my father is at the airport to carry me and Blue Eyes to the village where I was born.

I don't remember Christmas, only the gifts I have bought from the city. Only the drifting faces of family, of feeling frightened. Only sleeping in my childhood bed, knowing that there is something very, very wrong with my head, and my thoughts, and with everything.

It's time to go back to New York. Who can I tell? Who knows I'm swallowing double doses of Valium like a snake? That I am a snake; a liar, a sneak in my own life. Who can make it stop? I remember how Heathrow's toilets smell of digested fear; not fear of blood of pain, these waves I can still hold. What I smell now is vanilla-scented moisturising tissues, and anti-bacterial gel, and second-hand ear plugs, and foreign soap. I look down the toilet, hoping to disappear, hoping to vomit up an important organ, hoping to be forgotten, lost, maybe a missing person.

But, now I'm on the plane – high on my pills, ready to tell strangers *I'm frightened!*

The crew love to tell me, love to help – *You Won't Die Today! Everything is very Safe!*

I can't make them see. I want to die today.

But I won't. I will be trapped in this space.

Death won't come to save me.

We arrive back at JFK in a terrific snowstorm. We circle the airport for an age, but I'm too numb to feel anything else. There is an icy hour on a bumpy bus, as we skid back to the Upper West Side, and share headphones listening to PJ Harvey *Stories from the City, Stories from the Sea.*

We turn the key in our apartment door. There is a dead cockroach on the floor and a smell of damp.

PJ sings *This Mess We're In*

Oh, the mess.
I'm just a frozen pulse, with no blood.
And soon, I will forget how to act at all.

Chapter 4

Finding It

Back in New York, Blue Eyes is riding high. His face is in magazines, his voice sings to a new audience.

There are many nights, and drinks, and moments of sunshine. Nobody knows I am the rain. There is Polaroid beauty, and schmaltz, and as much glamour as you can ingest. I'm having the best time of my life in all the pictures.

I'm now working in the charity office, organising. I can process until 6pm, when I finish. I leave and turn onto Broadway into the dark early evening. The night feels as if it will suffocate me. My only solace are pharmacies. There are many to choose from. I walk the aisles, looking for the answer. What will get me through tonight? A new cherry lip balm? Vapourub? Glittery hair slides that are meant for a child? Or should I just get cough medicine and lots of painkillers? Painkillers from every pharmacy on the block.

And now there is another trip, another group, an airport. We are going to Tampa, Florida to watch Baseball Spring Training. I'm in charge. I have the black folder, its plastic sheets, the small grey first-aid kit, the paper bags of other people's pills and creams in pressed packs, my pen in one hand, and someone's hand in the other.

I'm spending too long in the toilet, while the group and my co-worker wait outside. I'm staring into a cold, traveller's mirror. I'm hoping my reflection might have disappeared, that there might have been a miracle. I realise, in quiet contemplation that I cannot pretend anymore. I can't ignore my thoughts, and move and act like a stoned robot any more. I want to get my pass now; the one that makes this all legitimate, the one that will give me permission to break. To fall down, to break.

We climb aboard the small plane.

And then I leave. I put all the things, the sheets, and the kit, and the bags in the arms of someone else, like they are boxes of bullets. I walk off the plane. It's not fear anymore. More solid exhaustion of fear, like rings of smoke in your eyes.

I find a telephone. I sit on the floor next to it, as if it can transport me to another planet.

I take the Valium. Oh, I take the Valium. I take them like they are smiling at me, little devils, being sucked down, one, after another, after another, after another.

I can see the plane now, through the window. Yep, there it is. They have all gone. Up, up away. In the sky now, hurtling towards their lost holiday.

I call the office. '*Yep, I walked off the plane. They are alone. Yes. That is what I have done.*'

My brain is still my own sick joke, my own terrible secret, a hidden cross-dresser, an adulteress, a murderer. I call my friend A.

He says '*How many did you take?*'

He says '*Get a taxi*'

I get a taxi.

I have stopped crying. I didn't know I was crying.

I am almost enjoying myself; I am floating through the window, in tiny yellow circles. I am over all of this (My Life Is Over) I don't have to go (I've gone) My bags are still on the plane. I am going to Harlem.

The driver; he charges me $40 dollars. Dollars and disabled people. Is this nearly funny? Is this nearly over? Can I please be allowed to break now? Being fixed means nothing. Nothing, as I float, no muscles, just heavy legs, arms weighted by purple sand, waves of warm nausea, hope a tiny breeze from the driver's African mouth. He says; '*Songs of Nigeria, tales of corruption, you are a poet, I see the future. Fuck the people, you can't help everyone, help yourself, run away, and get a new job. Things are nice in New Jersey; things in the US are free. Can you be free here? Do you know what you want?*'

Yep.

I want a bible, and a thick blue blanket. I want an angel's hand and a toilet to be sick in. I want my mother and my grandmother. I want reality. I want to be on that plane, doing what I am told. I want to go home. I am 22, and it hurts like two lizards. Just two naked lizards and then it's over. Just take me to Harlem.

A appears calm and under-produced at his apartment door. *Shit happens.*

Eat eggs. Eggs that swim. And drink tea from a Japanese cup. Then I must be sick. Oh, so sick.

We sit together on the bathroom floor, legs outstretched. He says '*I am honoured you chose me for this mess*'.

And what is happening here?

Everything is my fault.

The arguing. The constant arguing. Their unhappiness.

That wasn't your fault.

The crying. I was always crying.

That wasn't your fault.

The accidents. So many accidents. The drugs. Too many drugs.

That wasn't your fault.

I got run down. So run down. I didn't eat enough. Too many drinks. And drugs. And nights. And I got Arthritis, oh the pain. Everywhere.

That wasn't your fault.

And now I'm scared all the time. I'm scared of everything. And when I'm not scared, I'm so sad. I'm so sad.

You are allowed to be scared
You are allowed to be sad
You are allowed to be scared
You are allowed to be sad

I didn't know. I didn't know.

I didn't know. I didn't know.

What song do you want to hear?

Fake Plastic Trees.

She looks like the real thing/She tastes like the real thing
And it wears me out/It wears me out
If I could be who you wanted/all the time
If I could be who you wanted

And then he held me, because that is what you do when you have just saved someone's life.

And I say

Thank you.

And I return to my apartment. Blue Eyes is not here. He does not know that I am bleeding into the bed. My actions are already old news, I am boring even to myself. But this bottom of something, this fabulous hard, red blood-bath, feels a little bit like freedom. Because you know, *it is not my fault.*

Why have I been listening only to that one single voice of blame?

I'm scared
I'm sad
It's not my fault.
Write it down.
It's not your fault.
Write it down.

At the bottom, where do you go? There are no decisions about living or dying now, only actions. Shall I take a shower? Shall I take a shit? Shall I take more tablets? Shall I walk the pharmacies, walk them again? The answer might be on the shelves tonight. What will I fill this void with? This nothing inside, this space.

But, now, perhaps now I can feel something. I feel that maybe everything that has ever happened, was not my fault. That maybe, just maybe, the things I feel, somebody else might feel. That I was OK to feel them. That maybe everything you might ever feel is allowed. That you do not need permission, you do not need permission.

I write a letter of apology, and leave it with my work key and $200 at the door of the charity office.

Blue Eyes and I talk, and drink, and talk, and drink. I remember the singing from our Columbian neighbour intercepting our words, and us only stopping to pee; me in a saucepan, him in the sink; anything to avoid the shit and cockroaches of the bathroom. Blue Eyes sits, framed in his New York life, offering to take me home to England. But he will return. He will return, alone.

We take a cab in the middle of the night to a party. There is a sweet smell; the evening is white-lit and fresh. I'm like a chalk statue, drowning in another dirty evening. I leave Blue Eyes at the party. I buy vodka and painkillers on the way home, but it is a threat to myself now, only a threat. I only look at them in their paper bag.

I look at the paper bag whilst I also cower in the corner of the room, head by the window, waiting for the surges of panic to stop coming over, and over, and over.

I visit a hypnotherapist, she tries to take me back, waving a long, green crystal on dubious string and asking me where the pain was. I say there was no pain, it just all cracked at once. I sit up on her crocheted settee cover and start to cry. She says, '*Crying Is Good*'. She says, '*Stop Judging Yourself, Do What Makes You Happy*'.

I visit a psychiatrist, she gives me a list of definitions, terms, lines from text books. She says: '*You seem to have learnt to blame yourself for everything. You believe you are a failure, because you cry, because you feel. Who taught you this?*' She also gives me tranquilisers, the kind they give horses, runaway horses.

Blue Eyes and I take blue-and-white rimmed plates, a green plastic goblet, some roller boots, several CDs, a pile of books and a pair of trainers to the thrift store. In a thin Monday sunrise, we return our keys to the concierge of the apartment, who seems to have done very little concierging during our time here, but a lot of smoking cigarettes and looking cross, and he says '*Goodnight*', which is odd because it is '*Good Morning*'.

Heavily tranquilised, the journey home passes quickly. I even have a trip to the cockpit, where one of the pilots tells me about his severe phobia of spiders.

England swims up soon enough, like a long joke, only funny in places.

The next day I leave Blue Eyes crying in his mother's flat, after we have divided up our luggage, divided up the memories.

I go back to the village.

And what is here? My mother and father. I have typed up how I have been feeling, and printed it out, and I read it to them like a news bulletin. I have no re-collection of their reactions, but I feel as if I can draw some kind of line. I am out. Out the bag, out the cupboard – revealed, exposed, cracked. This invitation to be scrutinised gives me strength, because I am now, just myself. No pretending.

And there are still some of my things here, old things, things we don't know what to do with stacked under my old bed, in my dated pine bedroom. A porcelain bear that once had a scent, but has lost it. Cassette tapes. Tin pencil cases with names of boys scratched onto them with a compass. A My-Little Pony, which is still just uncomplicated, dead plastic happiness.

And I'm here.

I think of the pain, the physical pain, how I still stand with it, how I still overcome it. I think of the mental pain and its agonies, its unnamed edges. I realise how I have carried shame, huge shame of my thoughts, for so long. And now I'm saying my thoughts out loud, they don't seem so terrible. How when you speak, other people speak, and when you say the truth, your truth, whatever that may be, people listen.

So I talk to people, people who can help.

And I speak the truth.

And I learn that the blame game is for the really crazy people, the ones who love to bring you down.

And I learn that everyone is papering over cracks.

And that many people are pretending.

And I think of the participants, and their agonies. Their diseases, and diagnosis. Their rejection and segregation. Their scars and their cigarette burns. I think of how some worked, mostly in factories, lipsticks and toothbrushes, tinned foods, how they saved for their holiday. I took them on their holidays, and mostly; I gave them all I had. I cleaned them, and sang songs in the bus, and laughed at their jokes that didn't make sense, and took their phone calls all night. I slept with their skin under my fingernails, and this was a privilege. In the end, I let them down, but I know they would forgive me, because they know all about shame, and all about sadness and fear.

So I give you this. I give you this.

If you need to lose it, lose it. Own it. Walk off the plane if you have to walk off the plane.

If you need medicine, take the medicine they give you. You don't have to be a fucking hero for anyone.

Tell your truth, tell someone, anyone. Make someone listen. Tell every detail. Don't try to make it pretty. Share it. Shout it if you have to.

Cry. Cry as much as you need to.

Know that on every corner, in every part of the world, someone is surviving something that they never thought they could. Try and be them, just for a second.

The dark place is just a place, a stop along the way. There are other places. You can find the door to the next place. You can do this a thousand times if you have to.

Do one thing. It might be the hardest thing. Get dressed. Walk 20 yards outside.

Fear feels like it will kill you, like the adrenalin will stop your heart, like you will forget how to breathe. You won't. It's just fear. Tell it to Come and Get You. It won't, because it can't.

Thoughts like to repeat themselves. This is a trick of the brain. You don't need to be tricked. Welcome the thoughts, give them refuge. Hug them and squeeze them. They are telling you terrible things, but when you offer them a seat at the table, they go a little quiet.

Listen to music. Find the songs. Find your song. Hear the words.

Write what you can down. Write it down. Write it down.

Look for signs of life in you, not signs of death, especially when each hour of a day or a night are tiny lifetimes. Maybe a bird is singing. Maybe the moon looks beautiful. Maybe there is one thing, one tiny thing that can shift you into tomorrow.

Maybe tomorrow will be better. Maybe tomorrow will the first day of the better days. Maybe tomorrow will be the day that changes your life forever. Maybe you are just moments away from something extraordinary, that you could not invent in your wildest dreams. Maybe a story is unfolding that you couldn't even possibly invent.

The day will break outside of us, no matter what we do. It will break when we don't see it, when we wish it could stop, when we long for it. Even if we let it go, even if we don't celebrate it or mark it, it will just pass to the past, and another will rise up. Maybe we can hold onto more days. Maybe we have hope.

And what is hope?

It is just people looking for little signs.

People of the past, standing on lines of war and death and sadness.

People of now, standing in the same worn lines.

Looking for little signs. Little answers. A tiny single answer will do. Just one, single voice.

These people are not stronger than you. They are you. Keep your eyes open. Let's look together.

Let's look for Love if nothing else. Let's Love when we can't, when we are angry and when we don't want to. Let's seek it out. Let's be desperate. Let's be surprising. Let's say what nobody else wants to say. Let's only tell the truth. Let's be real. Let's find out that kindness makes us happy.

Love the strangers who pass you in the street. Talk to anyone. Talk to the old lady in the supermarket who hasn't had a conversation for a week. Talk to the people who you left behind by mistake. Look people in the eye and find what is keeping them up at night. Ask them what it is, because maybe nobody else ever will. Let's be sad and scared together.

And yes, how I miss those people I once cared for, the people that were showing me survival and love and hope, when I couldn't see it. Love for strangers. Love for strangers.

I long to wash them again; the moment, the running water, the underwear in a bag, the filthy tissues, the rubber gloves, the soothing words, the ceremonial rising up to some kind of God, whoever he may be. Because there I was, I was there, and they were there, and we were together, haphazard and glorious in the dirty horror and surprise of it all.

There are now decisions to make, and I try to make them with feeling, and relate them to what I actually want, and who I actually might be, which I haven't done before. I am moving to London. I get a new job in a prison charity, partly because my interviewer and new boss, a former prisoner herself, is born under Cancer, and of course I am too. We will be Cancerians together; emotional, controlling, manipulative, bat-shit crazy. She will tell me tales of drugs and communes, of re-births, of prison and of freedom.

Much of the darkness has lifted for now, but of course its imprint never goes. Just as my joints still ache, I will now have to work at staying on the good side of sane. I will talk to therapists. I will read all the books. I will even do an Open University degree in Psychology during evenings. There will be future dark times; new phobias, winter nights that don't seem to end. There will be many more moments of running away; running from a course, a talk, an interview, a journey, a moment. Running Away will be become a clearly definable part of my character. And everywhere I go, I will always look for an exit.

But for now, at this time, I am happy. I find some good things.

The prison charity have an office inside a shopping centre. These are truly terrible shops; mostly cheap women's fashion, thin fabrics, tiny dresses you would wear if you really wanted to make it as a prostitute. There are odd shoes; one pair sits in the window, month after month. It is there after I leave. My new friend T and I work out it has been unsold, but remains on display for about five years.

There is a grumpy centre manager, and a caretaker. A caretaker who slips from the transparent roof of the centre, crashing at least 30ft all the way to the ground. He gets up and walks, completely unhurt like a ghost.

There are television screens in the centre which show us planes have crashed into the World Trade Centre. We are open mouthed, along with the rest of the world. We are silent as the people jump, and the buildings crumble into clouds. My New York.

There are meetings for everything at my new job. There is even a meeting to decide if we have too many meetings.

Somebody gets very angry about cheese being eaten from the staff fridge, and sends many emails, entitled *Missing Cheese.*

There is a newsletter produced to send to all the prisoners, which features a staff photograph. I receive a stack of fan letters from male prisoners who *like my picture.* Most of them send a picture too, usually semi-clothed doing weights in the prison gym.

A prisoner from Jamaica sends me something that has floated into his prison yard. A parrot feather. I stick it to my noticeboard, I stroke it over my hands. I am transfixed by it. Then I spend several hours Googling *Diseases spread by Parrots* and convince myself I have *Psittacosis*.

There are redundancies. They announce the redundancies by ringing from the Director's Office. The phones ring around in a loop. If the ringing stops at your phone, then it's you. You are called to the Office. You are redundant.

Occasionally an irate middle-class elderly lady from Buckinghamshire will ring me to say that the work we are doing is evil, and we shouldn't help people who have committed crimes. I enjoy these phone calls very much.

I run a pen-pal scheme where I match prisoners with volunteers, volunteers who would like to write to them. On the interests form, our volunteers mostly like knitting, left politics, a bit of Radio 4. The prisoners tend to like weights, women and hip-hop, so it can be hard to find matches. We can't give out addresses, so we open the letters in the office to forward on. I find out that my pen-pal matching skills are better than anybody could have expected. I have matched a paedophile, with a paedophile.

There is a restaurant across the road called *Happy Days* where we get our lunch.

There is a pub near us too, where we can drink after work. My friend T leaves late one night to find a man in the doorway having a poo.

D, my boss and now friend, gives an excellent presentation about our work – her secret is to always take Ecstasy before public speaking.

I find somewhere to live, in well-heeled Muswell Hill. I'm in the bottom floor of a sprawling old house, with a huge garden, which contains a large fridge just for alcohol and is enjoyed by our two cats. My housemates are R, an old gangster with the coldest blue eyes, who has collected antiques and hippy stories from the 70s. He once took so much acid he saw only black dots for three days. He smokes weed like a chimney and has a safe with gold bars in it. His wife, F, is 20 years younger, and came from Turkey to be an au-pair. She is my new friend. R gives her gold bars on birthdays and anniversaries.

R has an inner circle, and you have to earn your place. I know I have after I am followed home by a man in a car. As I hide in somebody's front garden, high on rage, holding a high heel and my front door key, I hear the man exit his car to search for me. When his footsteps seem to fade, I bolt and race home barefoot. R jumps in his car and drives the streets to find my not-quite murderer.

Our other housemate is a doctor who has a liking for violent sex. R and F get married one day, with the reception at home, but their wedding night is all about our doctor. Her room is next to mine, and someone is causing her immense physical pain, which she seems to be enjoying. She is cheerful in the kitchen in the morning, making coffee and gesturing towards her bedroom telling me, '*It is like a fucking blood bath in there*'. I resist the urge to peep around the door and inspect the evidence.

R needs more cash, so turns the final tiny box room into a bedroom, by building a bed that is just a few inches away from the ceiling, with an enormous ladder to reach it. Luckily the girl who takes the room is a Ukrainian acrobat, so we can stop worrying that we will surely hear someone fall to their death.

Blue Eyes has not returned to New York. We have had a brief separation, but now he has re-surfaced in London, with a London modelling contract and band, and we are re-united, although he is living with some other male models in a Model House in Wood Green. There is a return to silly, glamorous nights out, and gigs, to his singing and his body and his pictures, and our endless, addictive attachment. We still drink and smoke weed, we still live without routine or plans, yet now I have a job, and must remember to wake up.

We have a very odd trip to Bruges. The driver of the coach to the sea warns us not to travel on the *Vomit Comet,* but we are fine. Our guest house, owned by artists, has a toilet that talks to you in Dutch when you flush. Our bed is made of white stone and is surrounded by dolls, many headless. We can't have sex with so many wrong witnesses. Or we have lots of sex, enjoying the wrong witnesses. I can't remember which one.

Spring comes. And then, as it heats into summer, things get very strange indeed.

I decide to run a half-marathon. As I have never run in a long-distance race and do no exercise at all, this is an odd choice. I talk my friend T into it, who is of similar sporting prowess. We train a little bit, we learn to run. I cough up cigarettes. I laugh too much to remember to breathe.

R and F decide they are no longer renting the flat, and buy a house a few streets away. I cannot afford to pay the money they require to pay for a bedroom, so I am officially homeless. They let me stay in a smaller room, for free, with my worldly possessions in boxes at the end of the bed.

Blue Eyes and I book a two week trip to Spain. We will spend a week at a friend's apartment in Madrid, and then we will camp somewhere in the countryside for a second week. But we miss our bus to Luton Airport, and therefore our flight. With no other flight options, we take a coach to Cornwall and spend a week in a very strange tiny holiday cottage on Bodmin Moor, near to the converted chapel where Blue Eyes' father and step-mother live. We are talking very little. Things have become disconnected and odd. I keep thinking of his step-mother's son-in-law who hung himself from a tree in the garden. The tree is still there, swaying in the wind. I have discovered *Ghost* perfume and sprayed it onto everything; so there is an odd sweetness to missed flights and the coach and the sad suicide tree.

We make it back to London and this time get a plane for a shorter Spanish trip. But there is still this horrible, cold space. Somebody stops me in the street to tell me in Spanish how much I look like Madonna. This has happened five, wonderful times in my life. Each of the five people who uttered the words, were convinced, enthralled, felt I was so similar to Madonna they actually needed to stop me. Blue Eyes looks away. *Fuck You.* We are at the general *Fuck You* stage.

Back in London, I run the half-marathon, get a medal, and drink some vodka. I don't know that after extreme exercise alcohol blows your brain, and I am absolutely out of my mind, very fast. I'm also on a bus going the wrong direction around a really shitty part of town, and then finally, after lots of *Fuck Yous,* I'm back at R and F's new house. I walk into the living room. I wonder why my legs don't work. It takes me a really long time to realise there has been a flood and I am wading through water up to my waist, my running medal still swinging from my neck.

R and F are now homeless along with me, but R has another flat, and we all move into that one, now everything in boxes, like strange campers. During this move, I lose Oops. Oops is a tiny red toy, half-bear-half-mouse, who I found on a street in France when I was 9. My 9 year old self swore that as I walked past his little red face, he called out *Oops,* in his soft French accent. This is my most treasured possession, and is now lost. I cry like a lunatic for too long. At least I still have my marcasite ring, shaped as an 8, which I found on a wall by the seaside when I was 8. I believed on that day, that it was delivered to me by a magpie, who knew my age. I had two magic tokens. Now I have only one. It's an omen, for sure.

I open the post at work. It's a Thursday, which I have recently discovered appears to be a day for unusual occurrences. As I open the envelopes in a civilised manner with a wooden letter opener, a white powder suddenly slides from one of the envelope all over my hands. I do the first thing you must always do when you come into contact with an alien substance from a prison; my innate clumsiness propels me to spread it over my clothes, and the desk, and my fellow post-opener. The letter in the envelope tells me that I have been sent Anthrax. There have been a recent series of Anthrax scares around London, so I am feeling quite trendy and like an astonishing insider, which has not happened to me before.

The men in white suits, with inflatable ET tube-tents come, and we are shut inside the building. We watch the road outside. The police are cordoning it off, but they have a forgotten a small passage behind the shopping centre, so there are a small string of people swinging shopping bags, walking right through the Anthrax cloud that I have released over London.

It's not Anthrax though. It's baking powder, so we can all go home.

But I'm actually homeless of course. And now, Blue Eyes and I have decided to split once more.

I cry for memories.

I hand in my notice. My boss gives me a voucher to have my photograph taken in Victorian Dress.

People ask me what I will do next, and I say I am planning to become a florist. Perhaps in Dublin?

So I run away to Ireland. I enjoy the loneliness of the drunk ferry. I arrive on the doorstep of my friend S, from Canada, and share his bed. I snog a famous person. I research becoming a florist. I eat more food than I have ever eaten in my life. I seem to have enormous new breasts.

I get the ferry home after a few weeks. I don't want to be a florist. I want to keep running.

Blue Eyes wants to see me. Perhaps we will give things another go? I don't know. I'm staying in the Model House, but jeez, I'm vomiting every day. I'm sick, so sick.

Blue Eyes is out when I get out of the shower, and faint on the landing, completely naked. It is another model from the Model House who throws a towel over me.

Blue Eyes is out when I celebrate consciousness with a dirty burger and chips, from a late night takeaway, that my normal obsession with germs would not allow me to eat.

Blue Eyes is out when I pee on the stick. When I pee on the second stick. When I pee on the third stick. When I line up the hat trick of double lines. Double blues. Definite Double Blues.

Blue Eyes is out when I realise I am pregnant.

Blue Eyes is out.

Chapter 5

When You Don't Want The Baby

My body works!

This is my first thought. All that illness, all that madness, and *my body works.*

It was working without telling me, it was working like a secret operator. When it got tired of being quite so secretive, it started to whisper to me. But I didn't listen to the whispers.

It told me to eat.

It told me my bra was too small.

It told me to stop smoking cigarettes, making me wretch as I lit up.

It sent me back on a ferry with an odd feeling in the pit of my stomach.

It made me vomit.

I was a bridesmaid just last week for my brother, and I know there is always a pregnant bridesmaid, but it was me. I was the one.

And only now, is the secret out.

Blue Eyes sits on the bed, holding the tests. He is also feeling triumphantly fertile.

But the miracle of biology wears off quickly. And then there is the shame of the mistake, the accident, and that is now flooding over us. Because we both agree this was a mistake, right? An accident?

And we don't even remember the time. We don't even know when the time was.

We are idiots. We are children, yet we are not, we are both 24. My innocent egg did its only job. The competitive sperm swam and then won the race. My body has started to do the rest, making an internal nest. We are fucking idiots.

A miracle was happening and we didn't even know what day of the week it was. We don't know where we were or what we said, or how we felt that time. Was it good sex, was there a storm outside? Or were we drunk, so drunk we were almost asleep? Was it worth it? Was that a day we loved each other? Do we love each other?

I go to see the GP. She is at least a decade older than me. Her office is scattered with pictures of three children, in various groupings. Baby faces. Older faces in uniform at school.

I start to cry before I even say why I am there. Hormones are betraying me, because now she can get under my skin. *'You don't seem happy about the pregnancy, is that right?'* she says.

'I don't know yet'

'You have lots of options' she says

Not really lots, I think. I mean it is not like some fucking menu of choices. This is quite binary right.

In or out. Yes or No. Alive or dead.

'I know I have options' I say. What I want to say is *Did you want your children? All of them? Did you plan them on a calendar? Or did you fuck up too. Is one of them the mistake? The first one? The last one? And who wants to be the middle one?*

She has booked me a scan.

Blue Eyes and I go to the hospital. I scan the waiting room for other idiots. But everyone here seems full of joy, and literally, full of life. Women at varying stages of pregnancy, holding their notes like certificates, complicit men at their side.

We have a little note to give the sonographer from the GP, explaining our unsure feelings about the baby. So the sonographer turns the screen away from us, so we cannot see what life there may be.

Blue Eyes looks at me, and I look at him.

We are ten weeks pregnant. The scan is *normal.*

10 weeks. *Why didn't I know? For ten weeks?*

The other couples are leaving with their grainy pictures. The ones where they can already see familiar features, mummy's nose, daddy's ears – when everyone else just sees a black and white swirl, a little blob floating in darkness. We are holding a leaflet of *Options.*

We did not want a picture of what might be in the darkness.

We talk for a week. We eat sandwiches in North London cafes and drink endless tea, and we talk.

Blue Eyes says a lot *'I'm not ready to be a father'*

And I say a lot *'How could we make it work?'*

Because in my mind, I am a mother. I know I can do all the things, all the things you need to do. So for me, this is just an equation, just an adding up of what we have, and what we don't.

I don't have a job or a permanent place to live. I call a benefits line to see what I might get, the answer is vague and insecure, but ultimately, means very little. My friend J summarises for me. She says everything would become a choice; nappies or your deodorant? Wet wipes or a bus pass? Baby clothes or fresh food?

Blue Eyes is earning money in phases, but he spends in the sunshine and does not save in the drought. He has just this odd room to live in, just a single room in a scruffy old house. Just a beautiful book of photos, and a guitar and lots of dreams and songs.

And us? We have had two break-ups and two make-ups. We don't talk about the future. We couldn't summarise what this is thing is that we have, and what it is that we don't. And Blue Eyes, well he is pretty certain, he is convincing and he is repetitive in his not-wanting-the-baby. And I would, ultimately be alone.

And I realise this. You become a parent as soon as you are pregnant, or have made someone pregnant. Your choices for them, they begin now. Whether you will follow the rules, and nourish your baby in your body. Whether you will drink and smoke, and not nourish the baby in your body. You choose now. In or Out.

And so if I'm a mother now, I don't want to choose poverty or uncertainty. I don't want to choose instability and a broken relationship before I have even started. I would make it all fine, I would survive, and yes I would do it well. But it doesn't have to be this way. I don't believe in life at all costs. I believe in choice.

I phone the NHS abortion-booking line, which has astonishingly cheerful music, but is never answered. When it finally is, I am told there is a six weeks wait. By then I will be four months pregnant. I gasp.

The lady on the phone says '*I know it is a long wait. It is usually best once this decision has been made to get it over with quickly, but I don't have any other appointments.*'

Her tone is cold and disappointed. I want to say *You do realise you are working on a fucking book-your-abortion phone line don't you? Who are you disappointed in? Me? Yourself? The NHS?* Or all of us. Just all of us.

My mother offers to pay for a private abortion which is booked immediately for the next day.

I'm given a list of what I need to take. The only thing on the list I don't have is a nightgown, I have only pyjamas. I go shopping in *Peacocks* for a cheap nightgown that can be used once and then thrown in the bin. I find one completely black and go to pay. I am about to pay the money, when I realise it has a word printed on the front in large gold letters that I have not seen - *FLOOZY*.

Yep, it says *FLOOZY*. I nearly went to the abortion operating table with *FLOOZY written across my chest.*

I go to get another one, but this is the early noughties - a time when everything seems to have a slogan sprawled across it. I could get the one that says *SLEEP* but that seems a bit maudlin, a definite nod to death. There is another one that says *DO NOT DISTURB* – and then there is a pink one that says *EVERYTHING LOOKS BETTER IN PINK.* Not abortion though. I'm fairly confident it looks pretty grim in any colour. Or I could buy the one that says *SWEET DREAMS.* Is this one OK? Can I have sweet dreams while they stop the life of the baby? There is also *BRIDE TO BE* which is perhaps the darkest of all, especially with the little red hearts everywhere. Eventually, I buy an oversize navy man's T-shirt.

The night before, I start the Googling. I read all the pro-life things that have ever been said. I read all the pro-choice arguments that have ever been made. I read about the fact it can feel like no-big-deal, just a sensible choice. Your choice. Then I read about the crazy women, wracked by a sudden guilt. I worry I will be that person. Somebody trapped in guilty thoughts, somebody in a loop again.

And then I Google the pictures, because the pro-life people, the pro-life men, who will never have anything growing inside them, love to post them. And I make myself look at an aborted foetus of 11 weeks, next to a 50p coin. It is barely the size of the coin.

So that's what's in there. A 50p coin. It is life? Or just the beginning of life? Does it have a soul? Will it hurt as it is sucked out? Am I a terrible person? Or am I somebody doing the right thing for my life? And for the 50p coin's life? Because it is not a baby is it? It is the start of one. It is not a baby, yet. And it will not become one.

We take a taxi to the clinic. I am hungry because I cannot eat. The hunger seems a bit of a betrayal, the life still telling me what to do. We are taken straight into the office to pay, which seems sudden and crude. I hand over my card and ask if they do cash back. Nobody laughs. I have crossed a line of darkness again.

Blue Eyes is given a room to wait in.

I am taken up to a bed with a curtain around it. They bring me the forms to sign. I sign. They talk me through the procedure. They come to collect me.

I lie on the table. I have had to bring with me a pair of pants with a sanitary towel pressed inside for the religious after-bleeding. This pants-with-towel lies next to me, a strip of indignity. And then they come, and they ask again. '*Do you understand the procedure? Are you sure?*'

Yes.

But of course, I'm not sure. Because who is ever 100% sure of anything? I mean is 98% OK? What if I am only 80%? Do you need some sort of estimate figure?

'*You are sure?*'

Yes.

And I think, please stop fucking asking me. Stop it. Stop it.

And then they give me another form to sign, and I sign it.

And they say, '*Are you ready?*'

And I say '*Yes*'.

And then they start to talk to me about counting backwards, while they administer the anaesthetic, and how I should count, keep counting

And I think *Fuck You* and *Your Counting*

And I think about 50ps. Just 50ps. Just dropping a 50p somewhere irretrievable. A drain maybe. Or into the middle of the ocean.

Or maybe when I go to hell, I can just keep dropping 50ps into the fire.

I wake up swearing, which is embarrassing. Because I cannot stop. And I want to say *Did you get it all out? Did it scream? What was it? Was it a 50p?*

And then I am sick. I am sick over, and over, and over. And it is the most cleansing and wonderful and complete vomiting of my life. Because I am vomiting relief, and I am vomiting choice, and I am vomiting freedom. And I don't need to be guilty, because this is my body. And my body is mine, and only mine. And if there is a hell, it's just a terrible, interventionist Man in The Sky who doesn't know anything about Choice and Life. And he can fuck off.

I have chosen to not bring this life into the world, because I loved that tiny life.

Because love told me to do the right thing. And this is the right thing.

So I will vomit and I will bleed biblical red oceans, and I will sleep.

And I will wake up at home. Wiser. Wiser. Wiser.

Blue Eyes and I are for now, just briefly, feeling the same thing. Regret. Regret, not for the choice. We still don't want the baby. But regret, that we got into the situation. That we have been living in a blur.

So we re-unite in a more grown-up version. We find a flat in Crouch End which is the ground floor of a Victorian house, with a garden. We fill it with some nice things, and we cook some meals. Sometimes we stay in. Blue Eyes models and plays music and studies sound engineering on the side. I find a new job working on a community project about healthy living. We try. We try really hard.

There are many gigs, singing at the front. New lyrics to write. Nights in Soho at private members bars, spotting the Z-list and drinking cocktails. A night of free drinks because somebody

60

thinks Blue Eyes is Ewan MacGregor. A night being chased because somebody else thinks he was in *Hollyoaks.*

We march with millions across London to protest against the Iraq War. We say No War. We say Not In Our Name. And we feel the betrayal of Tony Blair, once our student hero, who turns his head and does not listen.

I take coaches on regular excursions to visit friends or return to my parents. I climb aboard one coach at London Victoria, heading for Birmingham, to find I am the only passenger. This starts off quite exciting, but as we finally hit the M1 and I realise it really is just me and the driver for 3 hours, I'm unnerved. This would be a terribly mundane way to be murdered; just steered off the motorway, off into the nearest village, pushed off the National Express and strangled. Or imagine if there was a coach crash? Just two of us dead in the empty wreckage. Or if he has a heart attack at the wheel? Most of the drivers do look one sausage roll short of a cardiac arrest. There is nobody else to grab the steering wheel. I have no driving skills to offer. Or worst of all, what if he starts chatting to me? I put on headphones. He gets the message.

A month or so later, I take a very long coach trip to Edinburgh for the Festival, and to see friends. We are just near Glasgow, when I realise the man who has been sat next to me at the front of the coach for 8 hours is unwell. He starts to go into a grand-mal seizure. After putting him in the recovery position across the two seats, and checking nothing is in his mouth, I go up to the front of the coach and inform the driver. He seems irritated *'What's that love? We don't have that long to go'.* I check on the man, he is unconscious. A lot of the other passengers are tutting, they think I'm making a fuss. Everybody else is looking very deliberately in the other direction. He is shaking violently, his lips slightly tinged blue. I go back to the driver *'Call an ambulance now'* I say. He pulls onto the next hard shoulder. He calls an ambulance. We wait. Eventually it arrives, and two paramedics board the bus. They begin to tend to the man, they slowly lift him from the coach to the ambulance. They are asking him his name, although he is not really answering. And then, from the very back of the bus, at least an hour after this medical drama starting to unfold, an older man stands up. *'That is my son'* he says, shuffling reluctantly out of his seat *'He had brain surgery last week'.*

My new job at the community project is not going well. They have a lunch club for older people each day, and their heavily tattooed Canadian cook who loves double denim, has taken an obsessive shine to me. He is sending me emails. Lots of them. And then letters. And cards. And presents. He is waiting outside for me. He is following me to the bus stop. And it is feeling a little *wrong*. I don't know what to do, except talk a lot about my boyfriend, and how he is a boxer, which seems to help. I begin to realise I wish my boyfriend was a boxer.

I have also realised the project I am working on is misusing funds that have been given to it. I am threatened to stay off the scent. It is exhilarating at first, a B-list thriller. I come to work to find my files deleted, emails hacked. I go on holiday, and return to find my entire workload has been given to somebody else. Then it gets really nasty. Somebody actually snaps my wooden desk into two pieces.

It's a long story, but let's just say, I manage to get quite a few people sacked.

Elsewhere, Blue Eyes and I are dis-integrating.

We go on a terrible trip to the Lake District, where we argue with the owner of the guest house and are locked out on the street. He finally has to let us back in for the night, but I am convinced he is going to spike our breakfast or at least spit in our tea, so we get out early.

There are some very depressing rainy photographs of this trip. The writing is being washed from the wall.

It was never going to work.

Blue Eyes is beautiful. Beautiful in a way that when you wake up, you look at him lying next to you, and feel he is a work of art. The camera adores him. He is hugely talented too; his voice angelic, he is an excellent songwriter and guitarist. He knows a lot about zoology and wildlife and nature. He reads the books I read. He watches the films I watch. He is a fabulous cook. He is cool. He is calm. He is the cool guy to be next to, he is somebody the other girls want. People have started talking about *Metrosexuals* – and yep, he is one. He is whatever today is.

But his energy is not my energy. My mind runs fast, skims along tracks. I talk quickly. I do things quickly. I need entertainment and jokes. Lots of jokes. I get bored, quickly bored.

He does everything slowly. This was once endearing, but is now desperate. I start to test him. I ask him questions, but his answer is never enough for me. I try to get him to make me laugh, but the laughter is superficial. I'm becoming a mega-bitch. I'm trying to catch him out, and I'm trying to bring him down. And the worst thing of all, is that he would let me.

In my defence, he has become disproportionately self-obsessed. He believes his own hype. Every conversation seems to turn back to him, and I feel stranded again, like the only grown up in the room. It is me getting up for my regular job, and picking pants off the floor and checking we have the rent money. Our landlord, who is in his 80s, and likes to tell us long stories about his early life in Cyprus, only accepts cash. He also likes to wake us up very early on Sunday mornings when he turns up to mow the lawn. One day I come home to find a note on the door from him:

The police broke this door. Looking for Terrorists. I will try and get new locks. I see you soon.

I ask him when I see him what happened. *They said this place was a Ricin factory!* He says. *I told them no! A couple who love each other are here!*

I feel a bit worried. Not about the Ricin, but if we do love each other.

We talk late at night. We never really say anything.

He says things like '*I might go back to New York*' and '*It is hard to know what I want*'.

And I think things like: *You don't like Prince enough.* I mean that might be the measure of a man for me, how much they like Prince.

And I think I might have the ick.

Because when you eat, I walk out the room.

And I don't look at you in the shower anymore.

And you know, the ick. Well the ick, the ick is the end.

But I say nothing.

He stays out a lot. He's not cheating. But he's thinking about it.

I follow him to a party and play *You're so Vain* to the room. It goes over his drunk head.

But you know, who do I think I am? He is a nice guy. Everyone talks about how *special* he is.

The problem is my head which says:

We can't stay together because we can't stay together because we can't stay together.

I turn 25. I decide it means something. I forgive people under the age of 25 anything. I think maybe once you are 25, perhaps you should have some sort of plan, perhaps excuses have started to run out.

I decide I need a career. I leave the community project. I decide to become an archivist – I decide I will be happy amongst memories, and other people's letters, and dead history, and dead people. I decide it might sound a little bit romantic, but will mainly be about structure and organisation, which are my highs now, in these drug free days. I like tidying up. I like to arrange. I like to sort.

My friend S says that I have always been a ghost in my own life, so this is the perfect job for me.

I start working at a university.

I save up some actual money.

I realise that every day I spend with Blue Eyes is some sort of odd memory created, good or bad, that I will have to get over one day. That I will have to try and forget.

We are different. We were always different.

I've got the ick. And maybe he has too.

In the flat across the road, a man has been left by his girlfriend. It is a sunny afternoon, so he opens all of his windows, pulls speakers up to them and plays *Move Closer* on repeat. *Move Closer* is a great song, and for the first ten plays at least, I am all in. Then it gets a bit tired. After three hours of *Move Closer*, the police come. They leave. Silence.

Several hours later, as evening draws in. It begins again: *When we are together, touching each other, and our bodies do what they feel...'* Yep, *Move Closer* again. It is about 10pm, when the police come, and leave. Silence.

It is just after 2am when the street is woken. Yep, *Move Closer* has started again. And this time, it is accompanied by some drunk shouting and a bit of smashing of items. There is certainly no *Smoochin' or Swayin'*. The police come. He is taken away. Silence.

It is the talk of the street the next day. I discover I like *Move Closer* a lot more than anybody else, that I have a greater tolerance of repetition than most and that I am very sympathetic to a musical statement.

A few weeks later, I wake up on a sunny Saturday. There is a song on the radio, *I don't know why I waste my time, getting hung up about the things you say, when I open my eyes and it is a lovely day.*

And I think I don't need to feel this sad. This lonely. Because this is lonely, right?

And I remember the mindless nights back at university, when I wanted to dance, and he wanted to smoke.

And I remember when he sat on my hospital bed, and he cared, yes he cared, but he had no words.

And I remember when we sat on the roof of our New York apartment block, and looked out over the lights. And we said nothing, because we knew we were thinking different things.

And when we carelessly made that little life, that 50p, we didn't feel the same. I was adding up sums, doing the research, pen-to-paper; while he wrote imaginary freedom scores in chalk on his international walls.

We still look good in the pictures, but we just feel in retrospect, we are just nostalgia. Two friends, obsessed with romance, sick to their stomachs with seven year old nostalgia.

I say *'It is over'*, because he will never say the words.

And he sleeps in the lounge, because that is what you do, and kisses me on my forehead like a child.

And my work send me home for crying.

And he moves out, and we divide up memories again.

And I drink gin. And know this is the big break-up, this is the big one. And I think of how quickly he will lie in strangers' beds, and how I might still see his face in a magazine. I think how I wish I had the grace to *wish him all the best,* but I don't think I do, I want him to bleed. I want him to walk about with a six-inch scar along his back, a scar that is me, me carved into him forever. Because I wanted to be enough. Even though he wasn't enough for me, I still wanted to be enough. This is unfair. This is confusing. But some things don't make sense.

I'm going to shed skins. I'm going to tear them off in white stripes, and hold them to the light. What couldn't you see about me? Some kind of Bluebird, some kind of bird singing a song. I don't remember you laughing at my jokes. I'm funny, funnier than you think, you should have laughed.

But of course, he saw everything. He saw it all. I saw everything too. And we didn't want it. That's what people do. They measure up. Who is this person? What do I want to keep? What do I reject? They work out what is missing, they count up what there is, and what there isn't. Then they lie in bed at night, with the person they have measured, sleeping next to them, and they know the truth. They know, if they are in, or if they are out. They might say they don't know, but they know.

If you are out, do you stay or do you go? If you stay, will you settle? Will you cover up rips and tears and stains? Will you build fake bridges over voids? Maybe you will just hope, wait for change. Maybe you will hide, find a quiet place to hide. Or will you sacrifice something, anything, everything? Will you try and be somebody else? Or maybe you will just get really good at telling lies.

But the truth is the truth. If you are out, you are out.

You can stay, but you can go.

You can jump into the future, blindfolded, uncertain, terrified – convinced not that there is something better, just something different.

Something that you do not need to hold up to the light and check. Something you don't need to measure or criticise or try to mould. Something Happy.

And I've jumped. I pushed him off first, then I jumped.

The landlord takes my keys as I move out, after a few months living alone. He says '*Choose well, next time*', with a sigh. I have disappointed him. I might as well have been running the Ricin factory. It certainly would have been more fun.

I move back to Muswell Hill. My old friend R has an empty flat to rent, a top floor apartment in a nice mansion block on the high street. I find some people to share it with, two of them are my new friends, a couple L & J. It is a flat in which we share mutual love of music, a very dark humour and a place where we can be silly.

I'm also now at university again, doing an MA to qualify in archives, working just evenings and weekends, and there is a chance for regression. I find myself skipping classes like I always did, catching up on everything last minute, laughing in the back row at myself. I'm out most nights, I'm drinking and smoking, and I'm free.

I return briefly to the bad boys who I played with as a teenager. There is a handsome one with dangerous eyes, and a silly car he shouldn't drive, and a suitcase full of cash he may have stolen. He works as an escort – paid to take rich women out, take them to events, pretend to be their boyfriend, and do whatever else is required. We have fun. The fact he orbits a different planet to Blue Eyes deletes him from my skin, takes him out of my body as if he was never in it. Fresh sex makes you gracious; I no longer want Blue Eyes to be scarred by me. I'm happy to be washed away, in whichever bed he is now sleeping.

There are dates, and numbers to take, and new rules to remember. There is a very old rock star who really should know better. And then there is a multi-millionaire found in the Groucho Club, who gives me money to buy outfits for dates. Who chooses for me from a menu, and spends £1000 on a bottle of wine. Who wins my award for kissing, but cannot take my games, because I'm not really very interested in the money at all.

In a whirl of new affairs, Christmas arrives. My brother is with his wife and her family, so I spend it just with my parents on a farm in Scarborough. We get up at dawn to watch the celebration sun smile over the beach. We welcome Christmas morning with the sea, and with a flask of tea and carols on the radio.

This Christmas will remain forever, the greatest. The dawn, the light, the waves, the farm.

And in just six days, six soft days, I will step into the most beautiful night of my life.

If I could see her now, that Christmas girl, asleep in the farmhouse, I would want to whisper in her ear. I would want to tell her. The stars are lining up. I've checked. Only six days to go.

The sun and the moon are ready. Only six days to go.

Your childhood fields, your birds, your forest, they all know. They all know what is going to happen.

I can't tell you yet.
But the clock has started.
144 hours, tick, tick, tick.

Chapter 6

Mayonnaise

It's New Year's Eve.

My friend D, my boss from the prison charity is moving from her flat. This is a flat in West Hampstead that she once squatted, until eventually it became hers. After years of the nearby tube line shaking its foundations, the old building is fragile, and now condemned. It will be demolished as soon as the year begins. D wants to give it a send-off, and New Year seems the perfect time.

I help her get the flat ready. We are writing and drawing on the walls. She is sorting through a few final boxes. I find a tiny black ceramic heart that doesn't seem to belong to anyone. It means something as it burrows into my pocket. Or it doesn't. Just a heart. Just an abandoned heart.

The party builds. Her young son has invited it appears, the whole of North London. This is a time before social media, so it is quite the achievement. The MC gets louder. The crowds get bigger. South London is now gate crashing too. The building, held up by scaffolding, rattles.

I'm with some friends, and we are drinking vodka, neat. Midnight has been and gone. Yet, still more people arrive, more people squeeze into the flat. One of them is very tall, my first glimpse of this gate crasher is stooped shoulders as he ducks his head to get through the door frame, and then strides into the crowd. He is handsome. So handsome it hurts a little bit.

And I think *There he is.*
He will be mine.
I'm having his babies.

We start a conversation, Brown Eyes and me. And I think *This is it. This is the beginning of my actual life. My actual adult life has started right now.*

And I couldn't tell you why I think this. And it is not even a revelation, not even a romantic sweeping of my senses. I'm not dizzy. It just feels that this is a fact. That the biggest fact of all has exploded suddenly in my life.

Here he is.

There are too many people at the party now, and the building is swaying a bit too much. There are some police visits, something to do with a fight outside. A guy on the stairs with a bloody nose.

A man who looks like Jesus comes to tell us *we look beautiful together, we are meant to be together.* Either this means something or it doesn't. Just a pretend drunk Jesus. Or a real Jesus, the second coming, off his head and giving out relationship advice.

Brown Eyes and I briefly stand outside, get some air. And I think *Please fucking kiss me*

But he doesn't. He is telling me jokes, and flirting in a way that is oddly polite and kind and easy, and lovely.

Back inside, it is going downhill rapidly. My phone has been stolen. Somebody else has had their phone nicked too. And now, a laptop is missing.

The party's hosts are a little bit out of it, so Brown Eyes and I must stop this party.

I stand on a table, with him at my side. And we shout '*PARTY IS OVER! GET OUT! GET OUT!*'

We shout and we Get Them Out.

The emptying takes forever, but then the end and the quiet is a shock. My friend is defeated and off to sleep. Brown Eyes and I go into one of the rooms, which has nothing but a mattress and broken bottles. We talk. We talk. We talk. It seems quite reasonable for me to suggest that we get married. He doesn't really disagree, just calmly suggests we should spend some time together first.

70

We lie on the mattress, and we kiss, and we touch each other. And anybody else who has ever touched me evaporates like some sort of poison. Because this kind of touching is a drug, an insane meeting of chemicals, a kind of deep truth. And then later, he falls asleep first, and I fall asleep wrapped around him. I'm asleep at the squat party, in sudden and defiant ownership of my gate crasher. This is the one I want. This one.

We say goodbye in the morning. I have to help tidy up, then float home. I have his phone number on a small card. I write it on ten pieces of paper and hide them round my bedroom in case I lose the card. I get a new phone as soon as possible and text him. He rings me up and says *'Shall we go to the Zoo?'*

And I say *'What the fuck are you talking about?'* And we meet in Shoreditch instead, and we skip over the bar where he tells me a long story about throwing doughnuts, and we skip over the club where he tells me he doesn't like playing games, and we just go to my flat, quickly, quickly. And we have a lot of sex. And then we wake up and watch pornography with my flatmate because it seems like some sort of comedy rite of passage, perhaps an initiation test, and then we just go back to bed for the weekend.

The third time we meet, he is standing outside the tube station eating chips, waiting for me. I mean who does that on a second date? He does, apparently. He came straight from football practice, he is hungry. We go to a comedy club. He laughs deeply; his laughter comes from the deepest part of him, like noise from a void. It is loud and he cannot control it. It is the best laugh I have ever heard. We go back to my flat. We sit and look at each other, he says *'You are so pretty'*. And he says *pretty* like he doesn't usually use that word, and he has worked really hard to decide to use it.

The next time we meet, we confirm that he is my boyfriend.

And the next time, he hands me a little box with *Date 4* written on it – which contains a Prince album I don't have. The best touch, the best laugh and Prince. What else is there?

We have been together for a few weeks, when Brown Eyes wants a serious chat as we lie in bed, again. *'Have you realised I am a black man?'* he says. He thinks we should talk about this. He wants me to know what it is to be a son of immigrants who came from Jamaica. He wants me to know what it was to grow up as a black boy in 1980s South London. He wants me to know how it was to be a 15 year old boy, knowing that not too far away Stephen Lawrence, just three years older than him, had been stabbed to death at a bus stop, by white men for being black. White men who would be protected by the white police. He wants me to know about Stop and Search, about being viewed as a potential criminal at random, because you know *There is a man matching your description.* He wants me to know what black boys are told about being black men; about the role models, the choices, the baggage, the stereotypes. He wants me to know about the black women who might be cross he is with a white woman, and the white women who would date him just because he is black.

He looks very tired.

And I say *'Race is fucking exhausting isn't it? For something made up, for something socially constructed, it is fucking exhausting.'*

And he laughs, that laugh, and he says *'Yes.'*

And I say *'I don't give a fuck about any of it. We live by our own rules, together.'*

And we agree.

And at that moment, I have given up my pass, the pass I was born with that I didn't even know I had. The laminated pass with *White Privilege* printed on it, which was in my pocket without me realising. Because the world now recognises me to be in a mixed relationship, which means something and nothing, and my children will not be born with white privilege. So I must leave my pass at the door, right now. And when you give up the pass, one of the conditions is you must also give up white anonymity. Because non-white people don't get automatic anonymity. Without anonymity, you have to justify yourself in places and situations without reason. People will make decisions on your behalf just by looking at you. And there are now some places you are probably not going to go on holiday to (Hungary anyone?)

and most of rural England is now out as a place to live, but that's fine. I couldn't really see myself in living in Cornwall anyway.

A few weeks after, Brown Eyes, who is a graphic designer in a museum, must go to Whitby in Yorkshire to set up an exhibition. I travel on a complex network of overnight coaches and buses under a blanket and some slate sky, and through some snow, to join him on the last day. I'm in Leeds at 5am, which is sad and strange. I put on my make-up for the last bus. I arrive, exhausted and triumphant. I have asked him to book a B&B with a sea view. He has done this, but it has a skip of rubbish outside. We look through the window and I say *'Are you in love with me yet?'* And he says, to deflate my arrogance, as he looks out across the skip, *'If this is love, it is fucking rubbish'*.
And I'm glad I need to work a little bit more
Because it has always been too easy.

It is another few weeks after that, that he texts me as I sit idly in one of my MA classes. He has felt unwell lately, and been to see the GP. He texts *'Been to see the Doctor. I have the Big C......'*
I wait for the follow up text. I sit in the class. Nothing. I wait. Nothing. At least 15 minutes crawls past. Fuck, that was his way of telling me he has Cancer! My phone beeps. It's a text ....*Crap Diet*
I phone him up heart racing, fuming. *'Sorry!' He says – 'I lost signal and couldn't do the follow up text'.* My heart racing tells me something for sure, a feeling inside every fibre of my being that I have never felt before. Something profound and addictive and amazing.
Also, I'm really pissed off with him.

Easter arrives. I have briefly been to visit his parents, and now he is driving me to the Midlands to meet mine. It goes OK. He leaves first, I have a few extra days to stay. I say to my father, 'Did you enjoy meeting him?' And he says *'If you want to shack up in South London for the rest of your life that is up to you.'*
And I think, yep, it is up to me. And yep, I want to shack up in South London forever. That is exactly what I want. Because

I'm in, and I'm in deep. When I see his face, when I touch his body, when I hear his voice, I feel a stomach-aching, nervous, all over, sinking, drowning complete happiness.

The next week, I have to work at the V&A museum for two weeks completing an assessed placement. I catalogue the papers of an artist; an art-deco heroine, who ended up painting Butlin's murals and dying alone. I have to unwrap her wooden printing blocks from original green tissue. I have chosen a strange career for myself.

But Brown Eyes really doesn't feel very well.

He calls me to explain. We have been together a very short time. We have not been together long enough to trust each other's bodies, or even understand how they work.

He has pains in his stomach, and when he goes to the loo, there is blood. Bright red blood. Lots of it.

He is getting thin, and tired, and grumpy.

Spring is warm, and fiery. In the mornings, my room has yellow light. A year ago, I was asking Blue Eyes to leave. This spring, I am trying to understand why my new boy is so ill.

He goes to A&E. They admit him to hospital.

He becomes an in-patient at Croydon hospital, on a mixed male ward. There are many old men who gurgle and smell of salt, and a young man, diabetic and enormous, hooked up to machines that he shouldn't need. And there is Brown Eyes, braided hair tangling into knots, wearing a vest and tracksuit bottoms, long legs stretched out on a bed, looking both sexy and terrible at the same moment. It takes me two hours on the bus and the train to reach him from North London, and I feel like I can hardly breathe. When I arrive, he doesn't understand that this is what I will do for him, and that I will be here every day. He thinks I am just passing through.

He is going to the toilet eight times a day or more. They are weighing each poo like a prize. And he is bleeding. He is attached to an IV drip.

His family visit each day, and bring rows of snacks which pile up next to his bed. His mother says, '*Food is Strength*'. She tells me that she has cried at night, thinking about him here,

74

wondering what could be wrong. When I cannot be next to his bed, I send him text messages, and gulp air until the reply. I am in love for the first time; and because I have watched too many films, I am convinced that our tragic ending has arrived early. He will die.

He has Ulcerative Colitis. He won't die, but he is very ill. His bowel is raw and angry and bleeding. I notice for the first time that if you look into his eyes, his whole face seems to melt around him. Most people have gazes that break, that stop you looking. But you can stare right into him, and he doesn't move. His insides are made of forever. He is strong. And we do nothing else but laugh.

He has steroids and immunosuppressants running through him. At night he is connected to a machine to pump through the drugs, which he says feel like warm vodka. After three weeks, they let him go home. He has lost several stone, but with his new drugs is piling on weight fast, his face becoming round and swollen.

On his first night at home, I watch him fall asleep. My insides hurt, my ribcage aches, I feel as if all my energy has been transferred and as if there is no love left in the world. He has it all. I am checking his breathing. I have never been so happy.

He tells me that he loves me. He really, really loves me. He asks me if I would like to move in with him. I would like to. The world is full of colours that probably were not there before. We feel as if every song on the radio is for us. We just sit and look at each other a lot.

I say '*I'm a bit mad and difficult you know, and sometimes I need a lot of attention.*'

And he says '*I will always give you attention. You won't ever have to try and get it from me.*'

He is a man of wisdom and strength and honesty. There are no pretensions. And because of that I'm just a woman, just my real self, just my real, best self.

And bright, hopeful May turns quickly into June. Brown Eyes is back to work, carrying a paper bag full of pill packets and a list of what to take. He cries a little bit, about our love and the illness. He has survived a tiny personal war, and is more beautiful than ever. We like jokes that are about shit.

I graduate from my course, and get a job at the Guardian Newspaper, where I laugh a lot. We go to Edinburgh Festival. Brown Eyes has his first walk in a forest, and his first night in a tent. I go to Carnival for the first time. We take a ferry to Ireland, which is full of drunk men. We find ourselves a safe corner, where the other five non-white people on the ferry have huddled together in a silent act of security. We drive through beautiful countryside in a hire car that nearly runs out of petrol, and listen to the Greatest Hits of Lionel Richie. A B&B owner tries to refuse us entry, the big black man, and the white girl who has a really hacking cough – we could almost forgive the assumption that we are a dealer and a crack addict – but his sign tell us he has vacancies. He has to reluctantly let us in to his home. We also stay in a filthy place somewhere near Limerick and I get bitten all over by bed bugs.

Brown Eyes buys a flat in a Victorian House in South Norwood. I leave posh Muswell Hill, moving almost as far as you could across London. It is a bit of a shock at first. I get lost on a very run down street and phone Brown Eyes to ask where I am. *'That is South Norwood'* he says *'Where we live. The high street'*. Brown Eyes and his father renovate our flat, we make it cosy. There is an African man next door who seems to have a couple of exorcizing demons ceremonies, but one of the members of the 80s group The Pasadenas lives down stairs, and plays the keyboard cheerfully at his window.

We see friends, we drink and we dance. We watch comedy, we go to gigs. We stay in and talk. We eat out, all the time. We go to Paris, where Brown Eyes eats nine pastries for breakfast and we get lost and argue. Our arguing is infrequent; but when it arrives, is fiery, loud, aggressive, passionate and over quite quickly like a terrible storm. We go to Cornwall and stay in a B&B where the owners force you to talk to them and play that Jack Johnson album on repeat. The small talk makes you stay out all day, and get back as late as possible. Perhaps even skip breakfast.

I finally learn to drive. My driving instructor tells me that I have the worst spatial awareness of not only anybody who he has ever taught, but also anybody he has ever met, which seems unnecessarily harsh.

Brown Eyes has another flare-up of his disease, where at one point he refuses to even eat half a biscuit, but he manages to stay out of hospital.

I move jobs to work at a medical royal society. It is lonely and not funny, and I go slightly mad.

The feelings of old, the worries, the darkness would spiral; but now I have him, and he is a bridge that I can walk out on to. I can venture out. There is no fear of collapse.

One weekend, Brown Eyes and I are driving to go and look at a car that we might buy for me. We are on a busy dual carriageway in the middle lane. There is an articulated lorry on our left-hand side in the slow lane. The driver, sitting high up on his seat, cannot see properly through his mirrors. He begins to cross into our lane, shunting the front of our car, pushing us across towards the fast lane. Brown Eyes accelerates to move away from him, and then we start to spin. During the first spin, I remember thinking calmly *Oh, we are in a car crash* and watching Brown Eyes. He is saying *Fuck and Cunt and Fuck* and holding onto the steering wheel trying to stop the spin, and trying to brake with all his strength. And I am just looking at him thinking *He is a fucking hero, and will stop this car. I trust him with my life. I love him so much.* As the car spins, I see the frozen face of the woman behind us, who has children in the back of her car and is also trying to brake. As we start to spin round for the second time, Brown Eyes is still swearing and the woman is now open mouthed. We come to a stop. The woman has managed to stop, a pile up has been avoided.

People come to ask us if we are OK. The Estonian lorry driver is not very apologetic and doesn't seem to be giving us proper insurance details. Brown Eyes is raging, and I am worried he is about to punch this man in the face. I am relieved when the police come, when it is calmed down, when we finally get home. We sit in our flat with adrenalin pumping through us, because that was really bad. It was really bad, and we came very close to something terrible. Later, we are just exhausted and need wine and sleep.

When Christmas comes around, Brown Eyes and I are spending most of the day in our flat; we will go to his parents for dinner later. We open our presents. One of my presents is perfume, perfume Brown Eyes thought I wanted, because I had said I liked the advert. I really don't like the perfume, it smells of old ladies. Posh old ladies in a Bridge club. I cannot hide displeasure, so Brown Eyes says *'Don't worry, I will swap it'* and I say *'I'm really sorry, I'm really sorry.'* But the mood has sunk.

Brown Eyes decides he will bring his plan for New Year forward.

He goes into our bedroom. I hear the cupboards and the drawers being opened. I hear things being taken out. No tipped out. Everything tipped out. For some fucking reason, he is tipping out everything, he is trashing our whole room in some wild frenzy, on Christmas Day.

I go into the bedroom and I say *'What the fuck are you doing?'*

'I'm looking for something'

'What? Why are you making this mess? It's Christmas Day!'

'I'm looking for something'

'What for fuck's sake?'

He sits me down on the floor. We sit on a pile of clothes and shoes. And he says *'In a minute, I am going to ask you to marry me. But I've lost the fucking ring.'*

I start to cry.

'Where is my ring?' I am saying, *'Where is my ring?'*

'Where is my ring? WHERE IS MY RING?'

'Where were you hiding it?'

'Under the bed' he says *'In the drawers, under the bed'*

I pull them out further, completely further, with strength I didn't know I had.

And then he sees the bag, the bag that has gone over the drawers into the bottom lost place of the bed, and he pulls it out.

And now we are both crying, crying on our bedroom floor in the pile of stuff, with the open doors and the half broken drawer,

sitting on underpants and shoes and shirts, and there is my ring.
Two diamonds, a pink sapphire, and he says,
   'Will you marry me?'

   And I think of a little girl who sat at the top of the stairs when
she was supposed to be asleep, and listened to conversations she
wasn't supposed to listen to, and heard arguments, more
arguments
   And how I promised that girl that if she were to ever be with
somebody, it would be the right somebody
   And how maybe there could be a happy house, not a house of
discontent
   Not a house of sides
   A house of war
   And I say
   'Yes. Yes. Yes.'

   And we phone and tell my parents who are walking on a
beach in Wales, and they collect us a sea urchin.
   And we phone and tell his parents for a pre-dinner warning,
and his mother says *'I'm nervous now'* and his father says *'Are
you drunk?'*

   And later he tells me how he has a whole New Year trip
planned and that is when he was going to propose, on the
anniversary of the night we met, but Christmas Day was going a
bit adrift, so he thought he would bring it forward, save the day.
   And I say *'I think I would have preferred the New Year
proposal actually'*
   And he says *'For fuck's sake. Maybe this will teach you
something about patience'*
   And he is right.

   We begin to plan the wedding as soon as Christmas is over.
   My mother and father would like it to be in the Midlands, but
I want to get married in London.
   My father is hoping to spend as little money as possible, and
suggests I get married in the village church with a party in the
community centre.

We decide on a neutral area of London – Richmond, because it is beautiful.

Brown Eyes' parents think this is *too far* and are surprised it will be in an art gallery, not a church, and that we are going to get married on a Friday because it is cheaper.

My father says that nobody will come from our family.

Brown Eyes' mother is concerned that we have exact numbers for the ceremony and the reception which will be in a nearby town hall. Not everybody from her list will get an invite, although she would admit there are several hundred people on her list.

Both families become obsessed with food. We agree to do a buffet – Brown Eyes' mother will do West Indian food, my mother will do English food.

I have four bridesmaids.

My brother and his wife have their first baby due a few weeks before the wedding. She goes overdue by two weeks, so brings a 12 day old baby to the wedding. *Sorry.* We are still saying *Sorry.*

On the day itself, I have spent the night before in a Richmond hotel. I have a bath in rose petals. I get my hair done. We do our make-up ourselves. With four bridesmaids, I have five minutes mirror time and just wear my usual everyday make-up, so unlike some brides, I do look like myself when I get married.

My father drives us to the ceremony in his camper van. When I get there, I am told by the lady who will be marrying us that the best man, Brown Eyes' best friend, will not be at the wedding. She is enjoying the drama – a no-show best man! This might be her first.

It turns out he has *collapsed in a bathroom.* Although, this story is doubted when he is spotted at a party the next day. We never really get to the bottom of the best-man drama. We just know we have wasted a lot of money on a suit, and sadly Brown Eyes loses a friend, because an apology, an explanation, never comes.

My friend K, my chief bridesmaid, keeps me together, and I walk into the gallery to Nina Simone *Here Comes the Sun,* and we get married.

Later, at the reception, there has been a lot of angst about food preparation and setting out the tables, and arranging a buffet. When we sit at our top table, with our parents, food is brought to us.

And there it is. The bowl of mayonnaise.

My mother has brought an attractive salad bowl to the reception table, in which she hoped to arrange one of her salads. However, at some stage it has been hijacked by one of the Jamaican helpers, my new mother-in-law's friends, and they have decided to use it for something else.

This enormous bowl has been filled completely with mayonnaise. I mean, it is essentially a vat of mayonnaise. It is brought to our table. We look at each other, and we smile, and our thoughts unite in silence.

This my friends, is our relationship, our marriage, our future, represented beautifully by a bowl of mayonnaise.

My mother chose the right kind of bowl to look nice on the table. She did this with her English sensibilities in mind, she did this because she likes things to look nice. She did this because she cares what people think, and because this wedding has made her territorial. She can't help it. I don't blame her for it. She wanted salad in the salad bowl.

My mother-in-law doesn't know anything about the right kind of bowls. She is not interested so much in the presentation of the table, or what people think. Her Jamaican culture tells her that the most important thing is having enough food for everyone, having flavour in your food, and having enough sauce. Nobody wants dry food. She is feeling this more than usual, because this wedding has made her territorial. She can't help it. I don't blame her for it. The bowl was the perfect bowl to go mayonnaise crazy.

Brown Eyes and I don't care about the right kind of bowls, or the amount of sauce. We don't care about what people think. We are not chained to any cultural norms, and we will reject any that don't work for us. We know that we don't really go together. We are mayonnaise in a nice salad bowl.

And that is OK. We don't feel territorial.

81

Because love is not about territory. It is not even about common ground.

I have learnt it might only be this. It might just be this.

Chemistry first. You need to fancy them. Don't talk yourself in. Chemistry is Chemistry. It is either there or it is not.

Laughter comes next. Will they make you laugh till you shake? Till you hurt? Will they make you laugh at the right times and the wrong times? In the sad times? In the really sad times?

After that, throw away your tick lists. As long as they interest you and you can talk to each other, they don't need to be another version of yourself. They don't need to read the books you read, or watch the films you watch. They don't need to like your music (although shared Prince might be a good sign). They don't need your reference points. You don't need shared experiences, similar childhoods, families that match. This is all nonsense. This is trying too hard.

Are they kind to you? Because if they haven't been inexplicably fucked up by someone, if their baggage is not too wild, if they are not a psychopath, if they are mostly a functioning human being, then they can love you. And if they can and do love you, then kindness follows. There is no need for controls, for games, for contempt, for envy, for all of the toxic stuff.

And that is all. Sex, jokes, humanity. Don't get confused about status. About jobs. About money. About power. About hobbies and interests and opinions. About territory. Don't get confused.

Go with what you love. Keep it simple.

Know yourself. Trust your gut. That bitch speaks the truth.

She spoke to me on New Year's Eve. She had to shout over the drum and bass, but she shouted for me. And I listened.

And this one worked out.

We are married. And after the mayonnaise, there will be speeches, and crying, and drinking and brilliant dancing, and talking until morning in the hotel room, because nobody has sex on their wedding night.

The next day, we will return the Jensen Interceptor that Brown Eyes drove to the ceremony, and we will return

82

champagne glasses. And we will say *'Thank fuck the wedding is over.'*

We will open presents and cards.
We will honeymoon in France.
We will belong to somebody.
We will talk about babies, we will try to make babies.

And it is then we will find out what it is to fail.
What it is to fail together.

Chapter 7

When You Really Want The Baby

A few months after we are married, my desire to have a baby becomes intense. It is an odd, slightly unhinged, hormonal, biological pull, like an emotional magnet. I did not experience these feelings until the moment I first saw Brown Eyes. Now it is not just desire, but a longing, a weird longing to make something together, something to nurture, something bigger than us.

I give up smoking. That is the place to start and the law has now changed anyway. You have to smoke outside the pub, outside the club now. This seems outrageous at first; particularly as pubs and clubs no longer smell of smoke. They smell of sweat and piss, which takes a while to get used to. I have nostalgia for a bus we rode on as students in Leeds which was a *smoking bus.* The freedom to smoke on the bus was so intense, we would have to chain smoke all the way round the route.

I'm working now as an archivist in a religious charity. I have arrived as a professional to manage their collection, but have inherited staff who have been there for most of their working life. I will have to unpick their out-of-date practices and physically unpick their documents and objects. I will fill up bin bags to raised eyebrows, find dead mice amid artefacts and have to argue for new resources and new staff. I will work through a fascinating collection of social records that have been left in filing cabinets with mouldy tissues. Apparently these were used by a former worker, who had weeping pus-filled sores on his leg. I will become the bad-guy for some, which involves confrontation. On one particular day, my eccentric boss will actually hide under a desk when I argue with another member of staff who is trying to belittle my work. I will be asked multiple times if I am a

Christian. A member of the church who does not like my radical new heritage practices, will phone me to tell me that I will be haunted forever by the Victorian founder. I will stick to my guns until I get a brilliant new assistant, my new friend S who can fight the cause with me. We will curate a whole new museum. I will then enjoy my job, and I will laugh every day.

Brown Eyes is working as a Senior Designer in an agency. We have disposable income for the first time and we put our flat up for sale to find somewhere bigger. We are hoping that each month we might find out we are pregnant.

I have one of those knee operations.

Brown Eyes goes to Tanzania with his work and finds *Zanzibar* is not as romantic as it sounds.

We stay up late at a bar with friends to watch Barack Obama being elected as President. We are drunk and jubilant.

Nobody wants to buy our flat. The property market has slowed. The couple upstairs have sex so loudly I find myself doing that terrible thing of tapping the ceiling with a broom. Also our neighbours have filled up the communal areas with rubbish. There are many pairs of shoes on the stairs. We put them neatly in a bag and leave them outside our neighbour's door. He throws them back down over the stairs. We obsessively clean for every viewing, but we are stuck.

We are not pregnant. It has been six months. I go to the GP for blood tests. They show I don't ovulate regularly. This I suspected, as my periods have always been uncertain, each one has appeared throughout my life with sudden alarm, and after the blood there may not be one for some time. The moon doesn't like me it seems. I am prescribed a medicine to make me ovulate. This medicine makes me hungry and grumpy, and definitely not attractive. I have new spots. I'm like a horrible teenager. And now I have to take my temperature each morning to record it in a little booklet. When it starts to rise, there might be some sort of desperate egg, and we have to have a lot of sex. It is the opposite of sexy.

On the second cycle of this drug, a pregnancy test that I have peed on too early, shows us the lines. Really faint lines. We hold it up to the window. We put it under the torch of a mobile phone.

There are lines, but we can't be happy. Tomorrow's test will show fainter lines. The test after that will have no lines at all. We will buy test after test and I will pee like I have never peed before. We will buy them from different shops, different brands, in the hope that this will give us the answer. I will even pee into a little pot to test the stick that way. Give me anything and I will fucking piss all over it. But it is all over. Google tells us this is a *chemical pregnancy* – this terrible term, invented by someone who has surely never had one, was never anything that could be a life. Some chemicals nearly met some other chemicals, but they didn't. It was a non-starter. We are non-starters.

As the bleeding starts, my mind cannot resist its opportunity to taunt me. To tell myself the story again of the pregnancy that once was, not just chemicals, but a real, growing thing. That 50p that I signed away, the thing I said they could suck out. Maybe this will be my retribution. The moon is punishing me. The earth knows I gave away life.

I have to shout loudly over these voices. Re-confirm my decision. Look at Brown Eyes, and see that he, and only he, is the father of my mythical, fantasy chemical children.

After six cycles of the drug, I am signed over to the hospital. The fertility clinic is next to the ante-natal clinic, which is dreadful planning. They want to put probes inside me covered in condoms and gel, they want to inject dye into my fallopian tubes, they want to draw more blood. Brown Eyes must collect sperm in plastic bottles, and we must wait for results.

There is a hot summer outside, and we drive across France and into Switzerland. We try not to think about flats or babies, and eat a lot of food. Brown Eyes gets very confused in a posh Swiss restaurant and tips £70. We spend our first wedding anniversary in a tent looking out over Montreux. On the way back, we are just outside Paris, when armed police are at the side of the auto route. They flag us down. We appear to be the only car that has been stopped. What has alerted them to us? Our GB sticker? Our driver who is a black man? A black man and his white wife?

They want to know where have we been and where are we going? Do we have weapons? Do we have drugs? We don't have drugs, no. We don't have weapons. They seem disappointed and unconvinced, and the dogs at their feet are barking and snapping at their heels. We must get out of the car. We must stand at the side of the auto route whilst they search our car with dogs. They search for a long time. They seem confused not to have found anything. They open our bags, they pull apart the boot – our tent falling sadly to the floor like a hostage. After a while, you begin to feel guilty. I mean, I have been in cars before, cars that were full of both drugs and weapons, and I didn't feel guilty at all. I felt the rush of trouble, I enjoyed that high. But now I'm a grown up, a grown up married to Brown Eyes, a man with no drugs or weapons. For a moment, I wonder if they will plant something in our car. There is a flash of terror.

They let us go. Brown Eyes drives away, his hands angry on the wheel, but his face resigned. This is part of his life, he knows the story.

At home, the test results are in, and it's not good. My ovaries are polycystic, they are two blobs covered in little blobs, meaning eggs don't get released when they should; and the sperm, well the sperm are plentiful and good swimmers. But a lot of them don't have heads. They are fucking headless little aliens. That's what we are trying to make here – a random, headless alien baby.

It's been a year since we started trying now, it's been a whole year.

And I'm finding it hard to be cheerful. The trying, and the failing, is largely secret from anybody else. It is secret so we don't get told to *relax,* or told that *it will happen when we stop trying so hard* or *if it is meant to be.* But secrecy means we are open to a different kind of pain. Friends announce pregnancies. Easy, surprise pregnancies. Ultrasound pictures seem to be posted everywhere. Members of Brown Eyes' family ask Where are the babies? One grabs my waist and rubs my belly, she says '*A baby could have been born by now!'*

We know. We know. A baby could have been born. We won't tell you, but we are nowhere even near fucking conception. We are dealing with reluctant ovaries and deformed swimmers here. Please don't rub my belly. The only thing inside it is fear. Fear that this will never happen. Fear that I will never hold our baby. Our chemical alien 50p. A chemical alien that I won't flush, that I will grow into a £10 note if the moon will allow me. A £50 note. A bar of gold. A diamond. A blood-red ruby. I just need a chance.

The hospital puts us on an IVF waiting list.

In the meantime, Brown Eyes spends about £200 in Holland & Barrett, and begins a complex regime of minerals and vitamins. His healthy diet becomes healthier, his not-much-drinking, becomes no drinking. He exercises even more. He wanders about commando because this is good for your balls.

We go to a spa in the New Forest to relax. We wander about in slightly disturbing dressing gowns and eat large amounts of Thai food. We have massages that are not relaxing, but come as part of the deal.

At home, the sperm results are in and looking good. Some of the swimmers have re-grown heads, sprouted tails. They are looking normal.

It is just me now, set in abnormality like a disease. Set in abnormal stone.

And now there is a new feeling. It is jealously. It is racing, racing jealously and I have never felt it before. I don't just resent pregnancies around me, I hate them. I judge every mother I see. I stare at every rounded belly with contempt. I read stories of miscarriage and think *Who cares! At least you were fucking pregnant!* I have lost all reason. I have convinced myself that even a miscarriage would be better, just to be further along the line of creation. Just to be further. Less of a failure.

My Nan has died, and we must go to Devon for the funeral. We stay in a Torquay hotel with all of my father's family. We talk about her cooking and the songs she liked. We talk about her constant arguing with my grandad, who died a few years earlier. We talk about how they saved all their lives for a rainy day; and it here it finally is. Her funeral. Her money buys us a meal in the pub. We drink a lot because that it is what my father's family do. A man in the street asks Brown Eyes where he got his tan from.

Back in London, we have been referred to a private clinic. The clinic is expensive. There are noticeboards in the waiting room with pictures of a lot of babies, successful, longed for, expensive babies. There are a few sets of twins, and one set of triplets. I know I have lost perspective, when I fixate on the pink boy-girl-boy triplets, and long for them. How I would love triplets. How I would love three growing babies in my belly, fighting for space, like I am some sort of cat, plump with paid-for kittens. In the clinic, they talk in hushed tones and are too nice. The nice-ness makes you cry. That and the hormones.

The hormones that will make me ovulate come in syringes that we take home and keep in the fridge next to the milk. We are given a box for discarded needles, which awakens a deep desire in me to go back in time and re-visit recreational drug use with abandon. Brown Eyes will inject me with the totally legal and not-recreational drugs daily as we sit on our bed, and at first we will laugh and try to make sexy jokes. Then we will get sad and tired of the syringes. We will drive very early in the morning, before work, so I can be scanned to search for eggs. When the egg appears to be breaking through like a sunrise, Brown Eyes will be sent to the Wanking Room. He says the pornography selection in there is terrible, so he brings his own. His sperm are brought to the room, warm and triumphant, and put straight into my uterus, so they don't even have to swim. Then I have to lie there for as long as possible, with my legs raised, because apparently this isn't an old wives' tale, it is medically correct. And then we will go home, where I will take oestrogen, and progesterone – which comes in pessaries that go up your bottom like little rockets. I'm walking about leaking somebody's sperm and waxy hormones.

I say somebody's sperm – because I worry that the wrong sperm has been put in my uterus (I mean, how carefully do they label the bottles?) And would that be OK? I mean at least I would be pregnant?

I will also worry that the right sperm has been put in my uterus and it won't work.

I will worry that it won't work, all day and all night, and I will find I cannot think of much else.

We do this procedure a few times, a few thousand pounds. It doesn't work. It doesn't work.

We go on holiday with my family. On my 31st birthday, our agent rings to tell us that someone has finally put a solid offer on our flat. He is called Mr. Fox. We have had a beautiful fox who visits our garden every night, and it turns out he wants to buy the flat. Mr. Fox.

The next day Brown Eyes' brother sends a single text *MJ is dead*. We turn on the telly. Yep, Michael Jackson is dead. Actually dead.

We return home to view houses with such excitement, that we make an offer on every single one. Luckily, most are turned down, and we find a lovely, perfect one. We move into this little house, in snow, just before Christmas. We eat pizza on a mattress in an empty room. I feel this odd, spare domesticity that has no platform. I start baking a lot of cakes. Sewing. I still tidy, tidy, tidy in sequences, in orders, all the time. I re-arrange. I re-arrange the re-arrange. I touch things in circuits of three. Then start the circuit again.

It has been two years since we started trying for a baby. My jealously and rage and obsession with all things pregnancy is at fever-pitch. I make a list of friends in the back of my diary who might get pregnant soon, and work out strategies as to how I can phase them out before this happens. This at the time, seems perfectly reasonable. I have been following a strange ovulating-friendly diet for some time, and take all the vitamins. I still take my temperature daily, and pee on the ovulating sticks that smile if you can make an egg.

We get a letter to say our free cycle of IVF on the NHS is ready. We are lucky to have this chance. I decide to do something first.

I visit a Russian Homeopath in Chelsea, who has a beautiful name and is Homeopath-To-The-Stars. She gives me a collection of little pills to take, and also suggests I have a *Letting Go* ceremony where you *Let go of the pregnancy struggle.*

I'm not sure I can let go. Infertility is sad. It is hard, and it is sad. It has made me guilty and hateful and isolated, and self-obsessed. I don't like myself at the moment. But it is the failing, the constant failing of your body that does this to you. You feel as if you orbit another planet to the pregnant people, one that you cannot join. Your darkest fears tell you that you may never get to join. I see those women holding their pregnancy notes, their notes of expectation, and I feel only fear that I will never be them. I will never be a mother.

Six weeks later, the stick tells me there is an egg. We do what we have to do.

There are then two weeks to wait. A bit too early, I pee on the stick. I rush home from work and pee on a stick. I rip open packet after packet of pregnancy tests and pee on them all. I even have one of those word ones that agrees with all the others, *Pregnant*.

There is a really irritating voice saying '*Oh my God. Oh my God.*' Over and over. It is my voice.

I phone Brown Eyes and tell him to come home from the gym. This is basically telling him over the phone, because he hears the urgency. He is home. He looks at the test.

Pregnant.

But it doesn't stop there. Happy is still postponed. I can't be happy yet.

We are the lucky ones. Two years is nothing compared to the struggle of many. Those who go for years, who trail through what should be the best years of their lives, trying and waiting and failing. They re-mortgage houses, they let relationships fail, they become sad. They have cycles and cycles of IVF, their bodies and hormones and lives invaded with procedure. Some of them never get the baby. Some of them never get the test with the lines, and the word. Some of them don't get to be parents. They have to find ways of living with that. I am sad for them.

I should be happy, but I can't feel safe, I can't feel over the line, until the baby is a baby. Until it breathes in the world.

For the first trimester, I am convinced I will have a miscarriage. I check for blood in my pants, holding my breath each time. I have chronic morning sickness. I am sick all day, jumping off the bus holding a plastic bag, running up to the loo at work, and in the middle of the night. Only eating stops the sickness, and the eating is specific; salty crisps, toast, Fruit Pastilles and Jaffa Cakes at 3am. I have enormous boobs almost immediately, and become larger, larger quickly. But I am convinced I will never make it to the longed-for 3 month scan.

The weeks pass by painfully slowly. We make it to the scan. We hear a heartbeat, we see a picture. *There is something in there.*

We tell people now, but I don't really want to tell people. I am convinced this will be a jinx. There is nothing to celebrate, because now I feel I know that there is something wrong with the baby. It doesn't matter than everybody tells me I look beautiful (although enormous) and that the sickness has stopped, I am convinced the next scan will tell us there is something wrong with the baby. Something really terrible, something incompatible with life.

At the next scan, the baby is deliciously healthy. We don't find out the gender. The baby is sucking a tiny thumb. And now it kicks, and I put my hand on the kick and say *Please keep kicking, please hold on.*

My boss and I have to take a trip to Nottingham, we have to have a meeting about a new museum and clear out an old one. His driving on the motorway is a little erratic, and now I have a new fear, I will be killed. My baby and me. But we make it. We fill up the car with artefacts to return to London, which include an old dressing gown that is visibly crawling. The smell is extraordinary. But I get home safe.

I count the weeks. The weeks are long. The weeks are slow. I mean pregnancy is not nine months is it? It is 40 weeks, which is basically ten months. Almost a year. I still cannot believe that there might be a happy ending to the struggle. I worry that I will have a premature baby, one that cannot survive.

We go to Cornwall. On the way back, we visit Stonehenge – which is of course a terrible waste of money when you cannot even touch the stone, when you can just see it from the motorway. But I hope it will be bring some kind of luck. I don't believe in luck, but I do now. Send me luck, luck, luck.

I am now enormous. People on the bus ask me when I am due, believing it to be any day, and I just smile and go along with them, embarrassed by my hugeness. Even my wedding ring doesn't fit on my finger anymore and is around my neck on a chain. I'm an unmarried, neurotic baby elephant.

I go to the GP. It is a visit of triple embarrassment. Firstly, I am anaemic and the iron tablets have made me constipated.

Secondly, I have thrush. And finally, when he weighs me, he does a little in-take of breath at my weight. I have put on four stone. I used to think the GP fancied me a little bit, but not anymore.

I am sent for a pregnancy diabetes test on my birthday. This involves drinking a thick glucose syrup that is revolting, and then waiting around to see if you are going to go into a hyperglycaemic coma or something. I don't. I'm normal. Just really large.

I don't want to buy anything for the baby, because then it will die. I am convinced by now that my baby will be stillborn. But Brown Eyes does paint animals on the new nursery wall and writes *All good things are wild and free.* And we do buy a sling, a few clothes, nappies. We have a second-hand Moses basket. I pack the bag.

I finish work.

I re-watch every episode of The Office.

I do some cross stitch.

We have a new bed delivered. It has been sent with several parts missing, and is now half-built in the bedroom which means we have to sleep in the lounge. I phone the bed company to explain. The woman on the phone says, *'Do you really need all the parts? 'Do you really need all the parts?'* This is not a good time to be asking me. She cannot possibly understand how much *I really need all the parts.* She continues. *'Perhaps you could build it without the missing parts, and see if it is OK?'* There is a pause while I try to take in this information, while I assess the suggestion that we should just be happy, or at least content with something half-built, something incomplete.

Please send the missing parts.

Please send the missing parts.

She sighs as if I have caused a lot of fuss. She sends the parts.

I try to watch a DVD about breastfeeding the midwife has given me, but start crying hysterically. I realise that I cannot learn to breastfeed because my baby is going to be born dead. I try to think the best. I try to stop the worry. I cannot do it.

I count days.

Four days before the baby is due, I make shortbread. Lots and lots of shortbread, with a kind of shortbread urgency. That evening, something quite horrible called the Mucous Plug comes out in the toilet. I look at this blood and mucous and realise for the first time, I am actually pregnant.

Three days before the baby is due, I insist that we must go to BHS and buy a new shower curtain. I feel very strange in BHS, I have pains.

That evening, I have more pains while I am watching sympathy stories on The X Factor and crying like a loser. We go to bed. I wake up at 1am, to a satisfying feeling, like a balloon inside you has burst. Water is running down my legs. We call the hospital to say *my waters have broken.* They say, *you are not having contractions yet, so stay at home.* The contractions start. They are not as billed. They are not as promised. There are no gaps. Just one big, giant contraction. The hospital say, *come.*

We drive in the late October darkness. Brown Eyes takes a bumpy route, and I cry out for the bumps and the baby. The maternity unit is quiet. The midwife takes a short look at me, '*I can tell*' she says '*I can tell just by looking at you, that you are not in labour.*'

I say '*Are you going to examine me?*'

And she says '*I don't need to.*' I insist. There is a brief examination. '*You are not dilated*' she says. '*Go home, and come back later. Take some Paracetamol.*'

I think *You are wrong.*

I look at Brown Eyes and I can see he believes her. I mean, why wouldn't he? We are first-timers, and we must listen. I doubt my instinct.

We take the bag and the notes, the beautiful notes to the car. I think *I will never make it back here.* The bumps in reverse are desperate and painful, and frightening.

Brown Eyes is calm, so I must act now. I must act.

He fills up the bath. He lights a candle. He puts on the playlist that he has made for me. Kate starts to sing.

I sit in the water. The pain does not stop. I think of all I know about pain, about holding on, but I realise I am a fraud. I cannot cope with pain at all. This is early labour, not even that, prelabour, and it is agony. Absolute fucking agony. The midwife had said to take a Paracetamol, but there is no fucking Paracetamol in the world for this. Maybe heroin. Heroin would just about cover it.

I try to act for Brown Eyes. I smile as if the warm water is helping.

At one point, I get out of the bath and I stand at the top of the stairs, and I think *I am going to throw myself down the stairs, because I am useless at pain, and everything I thought I was, I am not.*

But I get back in the bath. But now I can't sit. I can't sit.

I stand up in the bath. In our mirrored bathroom cabinet, I see the movement, the movement of a baby, moving through me. I put my hand between my legs, and I feel a head.

There is a voice moaning, moaning, which is me.

But I am thinking this, and only this:

I knew I was right! I knew I was right! And now at least, this will soon be over, the dead baby will soon be here.

I am all powerful now, all powerful because I am right. I was fucking right. And I say '*Can you see the head?*' And he says, '*Yes.*'

And he phones 999. The voice is clear on the loudspeaker of the mobile, the mobile now on the bathroom floor. The man says what to do.

Somewhere in my village, the early hours of the morning are black, but there are stars. There are stars over my fields and my train tracks. In London, the stars are hidden by artificial light. And now the lights of emergency, rushing to us, blue lights coming to us.

Brown Eyes is ready. He has been ready all his life. He is calm. He is a goalkeeper. And he loves me.

He will tell me later that the head looked so squashed, he was sure the baby was dead. But he just did what he had to do. He just did it.

We look at each other just for a moment.

The glass candle Brown Eyes has lit for us, suddenly shatters into tiny pieces. Little pieces of it fall into the sink, the light extinguished. Was this the soul of our son entering the world? Was this the rush of the beginning of life coming into the room? Or this is what happens to cheap Ikea candles sometimes?

There are only two pushes, and he is holding a baby. A baby who is huge, a baby who is shaking his fists at me, furious at the injustice of his sudden entrance.

And now I am holding him, and I am clearing his airways. And now we have a screaming baby.

And now there are two paramedics in the bathroom, and I am standing in a bath naked and covered in blood smiling at these two strangers, as if they are angels.

They say to Brown Eyes '*Do you want to cut the cord?*' and he says '*No, I think I have done enough.*'

And we laugh, because now we can.

And they cut the cord, and they wrap the baby in their ambulance blanket, red for emergency.

And they wrap me up in another blanket and lie me out on our landing. They cannot deliver a placenta, so they call the hospital who say they won't send a midwife. And they are worried because my blood pressure is high and my blood sugar is low.

They call another hospital, and they send a midwife. She takes an hour to arrive.

She arrives, and delivers the placenta. She weighs the baby who is 8lb 10ozs.

And she sends me back to hospital, because I need stitches, oh so many stitches.

In the ambulance, I am holding my new baby boy. They are playing on the radio his song, my new baby boy's song, *Zoom*.

Faster and faster we were higher than high, for once in my lifetime I was finally free

And you gave that to me.

Brown Eyes is following carefully in the car behind.

The hospital does not offer explanation or apologies. I am stitched up by a brisk midwife, who is shocked at the extent of my very large tear. I then do the most painful wee of my life. Oh my goodness, that after child-birth wee.

Then I sit with my baby and my stitched up vagina, and try to breastfeed and do the first nappy. Brown Eyes disappears for a long time. When he returns, he has been helping a man in the carpark. His tyre was flat. And earlier, his wife had had a stillborn baby.

It was meant to be us, but it wasn't. Sadness and happiness on every corner. Every corner.

But this time, in this moment, we are here, the three of us. And within hours, I will be discharged. No need to be in hospital for a baby I had at home. My parents have arrived while we were out. They have bought a balloon and my mother has scrubbed the blood clean from the crime-scene bathroom and the new carpet. That is love.

And I sit and smell the blood and the milk, and the blood and the milk, and the blood and the milk.

And there is Brown Eyes. Holding his baby, like a hero. Knowing that if he does nothing else ever again, he has just delivered his own son, his first born son.

He likes to save my life on a regular basis.

And the saving will continue.

Chapter 8

In My Life

In those early days, the smell of the blood and the milk continues, until the blood, the bleeding of the entrance (or was it an exit?) fades, and all that remains is milk. There are pumped up new breasts, charged with finally fulfilling their purpose, that rise and fill to the sounds of crying. They feed the baby, which allows a womb to contract and close down its home, which twists and hurts and makes you gasp. And what do you feel like? Like an animal really, a milking machine.

And then you do all the new things that you must now do: the bath, the sling, the nappies, the blankets, the arranging of the cards, the folding of the new clothes. And you are so busy doing these new things, you forget to eat, or just eat biscuits, and there is no time for a shower.

And then the people visit. One of these is a Health Visitor. The clue is in the title; she represents Health and she Visits. For someone whose business is visiting, she has a distinct lack of guest skills. She requests that her tea be made in a certain way. She asks me *'How are you feeling?'* which is a trick question. If she were an honest visitor, she would say *'Are you mentally stable enough to care for a child?'* I don't think I should answer *Fine,* it seems too glib, so I say *'Tired.'* She sighs, almost rolling her eyes. *'Of course you are!'* she says *'You have just had a baby!'*

Now she has switched to the *Are-You-At-Risk-of-Post-Natal-Depression Questionnaire* which is disguised as more cheerful chat. *'How would you rate your mood?'* she says.

I have a vagina sewn together with thread up to my bottom. I am bleeding into disposable knickers. My nipples have cracked. I mean, how could I possibly rate my mood? I don't even remember my name. Now she wants to know if I have a *support network*? I don't know what one is. Is it some kind of system of

98

people holding hands who can catch you? I wouldn't want that, it sounds claustrophobic, like visiting that never ends. I try to smile a lot and convince her I'm not mad, and she goes away to do some more uninvited visiting.

After the people stop visiting, I look more closely at the baby, and realise it is here. It is here, and it is safe, and you must keep it alive. I realise that I was lost in the pregnant part, in the staying-pregnant part. I hadn't really ever imagined the having-a-baby part, not really.

My boy is handsome. His eyes are enormous. He is born strong; his legs kick hard, his arms can punch, and his grip is fierce. He is hungry. I'm feeding this boy all day and all night, and he never loses any birth weight, only expands and flies off the growth charts. His cry is loud and feisty, and the crying is constant.

A few weeks after he is born, I develop a strange itchy rash across my deflated stomach. The rash spreads, slowly, desperately – until it is all over my body, everywhere except my face. I scratch and scratch at my skin until it bleeds. The GP seems excited. *'It's called PUPPPs'* she explains. *'It is quite common in pregnancy, but very rare after birth. It has been caused by an allergic reaction to foetal cells left by the baby in your body.'* She is all over Google now, looking for pictures. She asks if she can take some to send to Dermatology – *'They will be so interested to see them'*. She takes the photographs and gives me some creams.

'For fuck's sake' I say to Brown Eyes after the appointment *'I am allergic to my own baby! I am allergic to my OWN baby!'* He is not listening. He has been checking our bank account which seems to be empty. Someone has intercepted a new bank card he didn't even know he was being sent. They are spending all the money we have in the world in Shell garages and on *Nollywood* films. The bank fraud and the baby allergy seem particularly bleak. It is November after all, and in the background is a small baby who is screaming incessantly, screaming without break. We go home and call the boy's new teddy PUPPPs.

Brown Eyes goes back to work, and I'm alone. There is a brief moment in the morning when the boy will sleep, and I wash, dress and eat cereal like a maniac. When he wakes, I squash him in to the pram and wheel him around the park, where he will fall sleep again. As soon as his eyes close, I run home, push the pram into the middle of the living room floor, and fall asleep on the sofa in my coat. Later, his colic afternoon crying will wake me, and I will wander from room to room looking for the answer to stop the noise. One day, the boy cries for five hours straight. I cry for three of these hours. After multiple feeds, burps, nappy changes, rocking, songs, walks around the block and dummy attempts, I decide calmly that I will abandon him under the snowy tree in the park. It is then I notice that a tiny thread from his Babygro has come loose near his neck. I cut off the thread, and he stops crying instantly. I phone my mother and ask her '*When does having a child become fun?*' And she thinks, and says '*I don't think it does.*'

At night, there is little sleep and despite having to get up for work, Brown Eyes shares the night with me. One night, as I am feeding the baby, he starts chatting to me about how he must get the catering sorted for this year's G8 summit. '*I don't think you work in catering*' I say. '*I don't think you organise the G8 summit.*' He looks surprised. My poor man is actually delirious with lack of sleep. It doesn't help that in a vain attempt to try and get the baby in a routine, I have made him write down in a shared notebook the exact time the baby wakes up, and when we feed or change him. I try to let him rest more after I realise he is cracking up, but I don't do it generously. Somebody else sleeping peacefully next to you as you crawl out of bed to a screaming baby is a form of torture. And I mean that quite literally, seen as it was used in Guantanamo Bay.

I'm aware that friends might save me from myself in these weeks, but I don't seem to have any. I didn't join a NCT group because I was worried I would become trapped in a middle-class-support-network but now it seems I might need one. I take the boy to Baby Sign-Language classes in an area posher than ours. It wasn't the best place to try and meet people. We sit with our babies on the floor and a song goes around the room. You say the name of your baby, and what they like to eat. My baby likes to eat banana, I join in. I thought this was a safe choice to add to the song, healthy, normal. The song moves on. I'm a bit doubtful that Baby Florence really likes to eat spinach, but maybe she does, who am I to judge? Baby Atticus likes to eat blueberries. OK, fair enough. And Baby Claudia apparently likes to eat papaya. I mean this mum has really raised the game. Fucking papaya! I'm a grown woman and have never eaten papaya, but Baby Claudia is being weaned on it! Jeez. The song is going back round again. I resist the urge to say my baby likes to eat Wotsits.

Luckily, two things will save our sanity. The boy now sleeps soundly, and has started to giggle constantly. Brown Eyes leaves his job to be freelance, and I go back to work part-time. We share the days.

Outside our cosy window, the world is titling. The Arab Spring has only just begun. Soon Gadhafi will have gone, and Syria will fall into civil war.

Amy Winehouse is dead.

In London, a double decker bus is burning on Tottenham High Road. Soon, riots race across our city leaving behind a line of smashed-in shops and buildings on fire. We sleep with helicopters circling in loops over our heads. The next day I pee on a stick. As it sits on the bed, deciding its verdict, I am watching news footage of a woman happily trying on trainers outside a looted JD Sports. I turn over the stick to see lines. Brown Eyes and I have *tried* just once, assuming the long, not-very-fertile road ahead. But the road was closed. I'm pregnant. Just like that. Just once, and pregnant. Our city is burning and I'm creating a miracle to join the anarchy.

This time, this time I can be happy. Despite terrible sickness that takes a long time to move on, I look forward to the scans. I feel happy at the kicks inside. I don't become enormous, and I don't worry. We have moved to the care of another hospital, and I have a sticker on my pregnancy notes that reminds people I may have a fast labour. People stop me in the street and say *'You must be hoping for a girl!'* And I think, no I'm not. I'm Queen Bee in my house, and I want to continue my reign. And I think I know what to do with boys, what to say. What do I have to teach a girl about being a woman? I'm not sure I have it worked out, I'm not sure I'm up to the job.

My beautiful talking, walking baby boy is now 17 months. My mother comes to stay. I go two days overdue. The sun shines and I'm fat and nervous. I go for a *sweep* to start labour (somebody needs to give it a different name, surely?) and after I have been *swept,* I walk a lot.

The next morning, the pain has started – again, just a single, continual contraction. Leaving my mother babysitting, we head to the hospital. The midwife examines me, but is quite insistent *You are not in labour. No labour yet.* We go over our previous experience again, but no, she wants to send us home. We refuse. She allows us to go to a gynaecology ward – which contains women who have had miscarriages. I have no access to a midwife or pain relief. I stand in a cubicle behind a green curtain, in the familiar agony again, and try to be quiet – because there is a woman nearby crying in her bed over a lost baby. I'm glad to be on medical grounds, but at this point it might be better to be in a corridor somewhere. Or maybe even in the fucking café. Distressing people eating their lunch would be better than disturbing those in grief. The pain continues and is intense. My waters break over the floor. A midwife comes, and I swear quite a bit and tell her I need to push. She looks alarmed.

I'm in a wheelchair in a lift, and then I'm being wheeled into a delivery room. There are several midwives but they are all standing against the wall, viewing me as if I am just a spectacle. They look bemused at Brown Eyes, because now I am standing up and his goalkeeper hands are out, ready to catch. Finally somebody believes us, and reaches out her hands too. She delivers the baby, who is just inches from the floor. The baby is lifted up, and I am euphoric to see another penis. This boy is calm with his eyes tightly shut, and his lips pursed as if in wise contemplation.

I feed the baby. I have all the stiches. I promise my vagina I won't do this again. I'm given a questionnaire to rate the maternity ward, and because I'm so high on having another perfect boy, I give them 5 stars. I nearly had the baby on the floor, but I give them 5 stars. I have a wobbly shower. The midwife says '*Is there much blood?*' And I lie and say no. I don't tell her about the clots that I have kicked down the plug hole.

I put on a full face of make-up.

And they say we can go home.

In the car, I'm in the back with my new baby boy, and his song *Easy* comes on the radio.

Easy like Sunday morning.

And I'm dizzy and crying warm tears.

We are home for lunch. The two brothers meet. Just a glance from the first to the second.

And I have everything.

Brown Eyes returns to work full-time. I am alone with a 1 year old and a new baby. Luckily my new boy is calm and likes to sleep, which helps. He also has beautiful grey eyes with long black eyelashes, eyes that seem to be river-deep in thought. I organise an outrageously strict routine which keeps me sane. I realise how rigid this system is, when somebody knocks at the door and I hide nervously until they go away. Spontaneity is not allowed. There is also no space for me in the schedule. I eat standing up in the kitchen over the sink.

The Olympics come to London and we are moved.

I return to work part-time again, and Brown Eyes is back sharing the babies, manoeuvring the double buggy we never thought we would have.

By the time my boys are 18 months and 3, I decide to leave my job at the strange religious archives. I will be at home.

My everyday full-time world with two toddlers is small. Our outings are only to the local shop to buy magazines and chocolate buttons, to the park across the road, and to two local *Stay and Play* groups. We wait for the groups all week; they are excited about playing. I'm excited about talking to some other human beings. Even the really boring ones. Even the ones who are still sharing their birth stories. Even the ones I would not be friends with in real life. One of these groups always ends with fruit in plastic bowls and song time. *Wheels on the Bus* is a popular choice at these occasions, though the group leader seems to have made up her own dubious lyric about *Daddies on the buses tutting* They *tut, tut, tut* those angry daddies at their own crying babies. Fuck you daddies. She then likes to lead us in a rousing rendition of *Free Nelson Mandela* (I'm pretty sure he's been free for over two decades) and her finale, *One Love* in a terrible mock Jamaican accent.

At home, there are naps, CBeebies and tipping toys over the floor. I play pretend-to-eat -pretend-food almost every day, which makes your eyes hurt with boredom. We read a lot of books. We chat all day. There are sick-bug days where we cry for teddies who have to be washed in the machine. There are naughty days where somebody refuses to do something and everybody screams, including me. There are sticker charts and consequences. There is potty training, which involves living in a floor covered with wee for several weeks, a poo in the corner of a bedroom, a flawed reward system of Maltesers and the biggest boy weeing over vegetables in the supermarket. There is The Gruffalo story, The Gruffalo film, The Gruffalo songs, and acting out all characters from The Gruffalo every day. There is a sand and water tray in our little back yard, which always ends with a sand fight and somebody crying. There is me, engaged in some kind of modern over-parenting, planning activities like a kind of deranged primary school teacher. Crafts at the table, cakes to bake, numbers and words to be taught. I'm making up for something, although I couldn't really tell you what it is. But mostly, it is just love, just love that I feel in these tiny days. I want them to feel loved; I want them to sleep in their beds feeling that the day was a good one. That we all tried our best. That they are safe. That tomorrow will be O.K. That tomorrow we will be here again, and what we have is enough.

All I hope for them is kindness; to feel kindness, and to be kind.

There are holidays with my family in Dorset and Devon. There are many trips to my village, where my boys play in the fields I once played in and visit the forest that lives somewhere inside me. We go to Birmingham to visit my Grandmother. For years her old age was defiant, and seemingly miraculous. She made it independently into her nineties with resilience, and productivity and super-human strength. Our reliance on her ability to survive, meant that sadly, we didn't see the signs of all the little things that were disappearing, and before it seemed possible, we noticed she had thrown her OBE in the kitchen bin.

She was being swallowed up by dementia. Now she lives in a care home, she lives inside her head. Small parts of her remain; she is still concerned with appearances, pleasantries, polite behaviour, she is still interested in vanity and in things of beauty. Everything else has fallen away. Yet, without warning, something will re-surface; a sentence that connects, an expression on somebody's face, the words of a hymn, a photograph from another time, a story re-told. In these moments, she has been returned to us. But then, the indignity and cruelty of forgetting will wash back over. She has left us, but she is also still here.

After a year at home, the big boy starts afternoon nursery at the local primary school. I have more time with the small boy who has never had me to himself. It seems as if we have reached a peaceful time. But Brown Eyes and I have a night; a silly night with a split condom and a not very accurate assessment of cycle dates. And then I'm here again, in these testing years, in these pissing years, weeing again over multiple sticks, in a different kind of urgency. We have a child about to be 4 and a 2 and a half year old. We have a very small house and not much money. And I'm pregnant.

Brown Eyes and I have never really been at war before. There have been arguments yes, frequent arguments. We are both fiery, and these arguments are fierce and vocal, but never about anything that matters. But now, this is a different kind of battle. He is upset about the baby. He doesn't want it. He feels 2 is enough – and 3 will break us. We cannot afford number 3. So he doesn't really want to talk to me. He doesn't really have anything to say.

I'm alone now. I'm alone with a mistake that wasn't just mine. I'm not sure I really want this baby either, but I'm in the situation and I have to make it OK. The morning sickness starts again, and it is continual and debilitating and exhausting, and now I have to do it alone, with my two small children alongside me. I count weeks. At six weeks, I hear the heartbeat. At twelve weeks, my mother comes to stay to babysit, and we go for our first scan.

Brown Eyes is opening a little. He is realising that this is actually happening. He is talking to me. He is here. I'm confident that the scan will make him happy, happy for another baby. I'm confident that the telling-of-people after the scan will make him happy too. The telling-of-the-boys will be a high; they will be excited.

I'm an old-pro on the ultrasound table. I'm used to lying on the blue paper that tears under your bottom, and the cold jelly on your stomach. I lay here with the 50p that never was. I lay here with the shimmer of gold that is a miracle mined-for longed-for first-born baby. I lay here with a little secret diamond, the second baby that came as a surprise, shiny and untainted. And now I'm here with this one, what is this one? What is in there? The image floats up on the screen.

In there, is something curled into a ball. Curled into a tight, eyes closed, ball. I've seen that tight curled ball before. I remember my childhood kitten, the one that was hit on the road, perfect in death. Curled up in protection. Or was it curled up in pain, some kind of surrender? And just a few weeks ago, I saw the same thing again. This time a baby fox, outside on our road, also curled inwards, also curled into itself. I pushed the buggy past it and hid tears from my children. The baby fox was just a baby, too beautiful and new to be at the side of the road amongst the rubbish and the people who didn't see it. On that day, Kate sang in my head for the rest of the day. *I found a fox, caught by dogs, He let me take him in my hands, His little heart, it beats so fast.*

The sonographer is young, a new one. Too young for bad news. *'I'm sorry'* he says *'There is no heartbeat. The baby died some time ago'.*

And I think *We can't go back. A heart cannot be re-started. Only I heard that heartbeat, only I and a midwife who will have forgotten it, as she works in heartbeats. I heard it. But it stopped.*

And I say *'When did it die?'* And he says *'I think about nine weeks.'*

And I think, I have had a dead baby inside me for three weeks. What kind of mother am I? Why didn't I know the heart had stopped? Why didn't I feel it? When it stopped, what was I

106

doing? Was I looking at the sky? Was I telling the children I loved them in their beds? Or was I sat on the toilet? Was I boiling pasta in the kitchen? Was I asleep?

And Kate sings to me again, and she says *Here I go, it's coming for me through the trees, help me someone, help me please.*

And I look at Brown Eyes. There is only one thing on his face. Relief.

And we are sent to the Gone-Wrong Room. Away from the Happy Pregnant-People-Room, to the Gone-Wrong Room. The walls are lilac and there are tissues, so there must have been a death. But what died? It was smaller than the 50p after all. It was a 20p. A 20p I found in my pocket, a 20p I kept turning over in my hand. A 20p that I would have loved and grown into a jewel, just like the others. But for Brown Eyes, it was small change, an inconvenience, a dirty coin.

It's called a missed-miscarriage they say. And I think, who missed it? Surely it was me, the mother that did the missing. I'm told to come back to hospital the next day, to have it removed.

I'm there in the early morning. I'm dressed in a gown, and I wait, alone again. It's just a few days before Christmas, and I can hear Christmas songs somewhere on a radio. There is another black anaesthetic, and then the rising up, and more blood, and then getting dressed. Then Brown Eyes and two boys in a car. And I have to forgive Brown Eyes because he couldn't pretend. And I have to forgive myself, although I don't know how to. And we have to be normal and eat, because we have children, real children. We stop outside the fish and chip shop, Brown Eyes goes inside to get food. My telephone rings, it is my father. My mother returned home from us today. She returned to news from her brother, my grandmother is ill. And then quickly, this afternoon, my grandmother is dead.

Where did she go? She believed in her soul, she believed it. Her soul would rise up, rise up to somewhere. Did she rise up as I lay on the table? As they put my legs in stirrups, as they sucked out and scraped out my womb, as they took out a little life? Did two deaths really coincide like some kind of terrible made-for-TV movie? Or was my 20p not enough? Just small change in the tides of life and death. Because I can't expect my 20p to have a soul if I was sure my 50p didn't. I can't change the rules. But my grandmother, she did. Yes, she did. There was something so fierce and bright and strong, and it must live somewhere now, it must live. And these tears now are my tears of relief for her, for peace. My tears for life and death, and the mystery, the strange mystery of a heart that beats, or stops. A nine week old heart. A 98 year old heart. Hearts that stop. That's what they do. They stop.

There is a black, cold Christmas, but then days carry us on. The small child-days which are long, which make you cry for their bedtime. Then once they are in bed, I feel sad for the days that go, for their growing that is flying past, as they move slowly away from you. And then I wake into another long day, and cannot remember sadness, until it returns later. In time, the big boy starts school, and the small boy starts nursery in the mornings. And it is not long, before the small boy starts school too.

My early work is completed, a kind of investment project. I've had thousands of hours with them, and I'm lucky, so very lucky. With both at school, I return to work, getting a new job quickly, three days a week in a university archive in the East-End.

The return to work makes us think we can buy a new house, our house is lovely, but tiny. We get an offer quickly, and then realise we cannot actually afford what we thought. We have to find something both bigger and cheaper than our current house, which is like being trapped in some kind of comedy riddle. In desperation, we view some strange places and try to buy them all. Our children are not convinced. One of them has a fat man with an oxygen mask, who is still managing to smoke a cigarette, and I think they think he comes with the house. Eventually, we buy a large Edwardian Crystal Palace house that is falling to pieces.

Brown Eyes and his father set about the enormous task of renovating it room by room. It starts with not having a kitchen for six months. It challenges every tidy obsession and clean ritual

I live by, and I end up surviving it by seeing it as some sort of Cognitive Behavioural Therapy.

And now, I'm in my life. I'm here, and I'm in it.

Football. Learning to swim. Learning to ride bikes. Talking to mums at the school gate. Parks and playgrounds. Drawing and writing. Games. Lists of plans in every summer holiday. Birthdays with friends. Stressful homemade birthday cakes. Number balloons. Sleepless Christmas nights. Center Parcs holidays. Holidays in Wales and Scotland. Pizza Express. Museums. Endless books. Endless pasta. Brotherly fights. Chicken Pox. Parent's evenings. School assemblies. Tea and biscuits.

Prince is dead.
Britain votes to leave Europe.

We are both working hard. The children, the jobs, the house to fix. Just a normal life, some normal people.

But something is not right. What is it?

I have to get up at 5am on my work days, I have a long commute, and I'm not enjoying it. The journey or the job. But it is sliding out of perspective, and I couldn't explain why. My brain is trying to tell me something. Sometimes I find myself walking, just walking for miles, wandering home in painful shoes, trying to walk something away, trying to find something out.

The house is becoming a home; the kitchen finished, the boys' rooms are cosy and complete, a new bathroom is looking beautiful. But it doesn't seem to mean anything. My brain is trying to talk to me, but I don't know what it is saying. Why don't I feel anything?

I start to wake up in the night, always the same time, around 1am. I wake up with immediacy, bolt upright, a jolt out of sleep. And I feel a sudden and catastrophic foreboding, like something truly terrible is about to happen. My brain is sending a signal, but I don't understand it. What is going to happen? Why am I afraid?

I think I'm tired, I'm just tired. So after two years, I decide to hand my notice in at my job. I'm going to do something different? What will I be? What will I be when I grow up?

I turn 40. Brown Eyes makes me a lovely book with messages from all my friends as if I am dead.

I wonder perhaps if I am going mad again. I wonder perhaps if this time, this time will be the real madness, the real losing it. Because my brain feels as if it is on a loop, and I cannot stop the loop.

It's the end of summer holidays, it's the last week. There has been a sunny day playing football in the park. Everybody has gone to bed happy. We say *Sweet Dreams* and *I Love you* and *God Bless.*

I sleep. I'm so tired.

I remember I was dreaming, I think it was a nice dream. As a child, I used to dream I was jumping through windows, window after window smashing behind me. Often these days, I dream I am in a huge room full of rows of dirty toilets where I can't find my way out. Sometimes I dream about Blue Eyes, I haven't spoken to him for years, but he swims up in dreams, asking me questions that I cannot answer, and I'm sad when I wake up. Sometimes I dream about playing *Murder in the Dark* which we used to play with my cousins as a child. You tip-toed around our dark house, and when the chosen Murderer tapped you on the shoulder, you fell to the floor screaming.

I don't know what I was dreaming about on this night. I hope it was a nice dream, because these will be my last moments of sleep in this life, in this normal life.

I know it is 1am when my brain wakes me up. It is always 1am. And this time, my brain is finally tired of trying to talk to me. I haven't been listening. It's been tapping me on the shoulder asking me to scream for months, and I haven't been playing the game. I haven't been murdered in the dark.

My village does not remember me. The birds, the crops, the skies – they are all different, a new generation. Who knows the story now? Maybe an urban fox outside in the bins, the furious magpies on the broken fence, or the London parakeets, rebel descendants of an escape artist.

So my brain will have to do the only thing it can; it's going to set off an electrical storm.

I won't remember the sparks.

I will remember a paramedic in my un-decorated bedroom, and Brown Eyes saying the word seizure. I will remember an ambulance flashing blue as I try to talk. Try to ask if I'm having a stroke.

I will remember bright A&E lights, and blood pouring out of my mouth.

And I will remember words, words from strangers, words about my brain.

My brain and all of its secrets.
I'm listening now, I'm listening.
Tell me what's wrong. Tell me everything.

Chapter 9

In My Brain

I'm in the hospital. I'm in the emergency part of the hospital.

I've had five seizures now. Five epic seizures without a break. Five storms. Five earthquakes.

Brown Eyes is next to the bed. It is the middle of the night and he has taken the boys to his parents. The doctors are asking him questions, questions about me. *Did she take drugs tonight? Did she take drugs tonight? Did she take drugs tonight?*

'No', he says. 'No. No.'

Did I take drugs tonight? No. That was somebody I used to be. *Who am I now? What happened?*

Has she had any recent personality changes?

'No' he says. No. Only we both know that the answer is yes. It is always yes. I've been going through personalities without any regard for reality my whole life. I couldn't even remember all the people who I have been. I don't even know who I was last week.

'*When was your last period?*' Somebody is saying '*When was your last period?*' And I think, Jeez I could never answer that question, I have never known the answer to that question. Especially not now, because I cannot speak right now. I open my mouth, but I cannot speak. And if I could, I wouldn't waste my words on periods. I would say *Help* or *Save Me, Just Save Me.*

And now here come the drugs; a beautiful injection in my arm to stop the storms, to stop the earthquakes, to bring me back. I'm in a CT scan just for a moment, and then back under the darkness, the black sleep. Then I'm in the MRI scanner. What time is it? What do the beeps mean? Is it dawn yet? Is my brain smiling to you on the pictures in a new dawn?

I'm coming up from the sleep again, I'm back in the bed. And I'm thinking about a book I read recently about imaginary illnesses, psychosomatic illness. And in this book, people had

112

seizures, they had real seizures with only psychological cause. And I think, *fuck, that's me. I'm now so mental, so unhinged, such a bat-shit crazy bitch I'm actually having psycho seizures.* The Doctor comes to talk to Brown Eyes and me. She says '*There is a mass on your brain. A mass.'*

And I think about the mass. A lump. A piece. A portion. A section. A body. Something of considerable quantity. Of volume. Like a crowd, a cheering crowd, a mass at the rave, taking the drugs tonight. A mass. An expanse. A void.

A mass. A mass in a cathedral. A solemn requiem. A song from my brain, singing with the choir, singing the gospel. A mass for the dead.

A tumour.

And I think *I have a brain tumour. Thank God, It wasn't psycho-seizures. This is legitimate. I'm legitimate. This is a legitimate situation.*

I'm moved from the emergency bit, because I'm legitimate and diagnosed, to the bit called the High Dependency Unit. In the bed next to me is my favourite actress, who was recently nominated for an Oscar. We chat. We chat for hours. The Doctor comes and says '*We need to move you to a neurological ward, but you two are getting on so well, you can stay here.'* This is like a line from a medical soap opera, where doctors have the time to get freely involved in patients personal lives, but it really happened. We talk some more.

Brown Eyes comes and says '*Do you think this whole brain tumour thing was so you could meet her and become friends?'* And I say '*Yes, probably.'*

The Doctor comes back to say that my brain tumour is not benign. It is cancer. I have brain cancer. I turn to Brown Eyes and say '*Please remember that when I am dead, you do not have my permission to be happy. I will fucking haunt you. Is that OK?'*

'*It depends if you are a sexy ghost',* he says.

After two nights, I am sent home from hospital with my brain full of cancer, some steroids and some anti-seizure medicine. We arrive home. On the doormat, is an ominous looking brown envelope addressed to the elderly man, now dead, who used to live in this house with his wife. I open it. It's a leaflet from a company who have not accepted the digital age. They are still selling pornography on DVDs and even videos. The leaflet is a graphic booklet of what they offer, and it seems that Brian had been an enthusiastic customer within a particular niche genre. I have a steady browse through pictures of people in their eighties and nineties having extremely graphic things done to them by people in their twenties. Some of them have even got their pets involved. Thanks Brian. Thanks for making the Day of Brain Cancer about something else. Thanks for filling the tumour with images of bestiality and a middle aged woman giving a toothless old man a blow job.

Brown Eyes phones my parents to tell them the news. We talk to our boys who are 6 and 7. We say *'Mummy has brain cancer that is why she had seizures. We don't know what will happen, but if you are worried about anything, just talk to us.'*
And they say calmly, *'Will you die Mummy?'*
And I say *'I might do. I will try not to, but I might do. But remember, anybody can die. We don't know when anybody will die. That is why we are always happy for the day we have. Today. Be happy for today.'*
My parents arrive. We behave as we normally would. I'm cooking for everyone. My father suggests we all go on a trip on the London Eye. Nobody responds to this suggestion. Where do you even start with a reply? They stay a little while. Once they are back home, my father sends unsolicited Brain Cancer email updates to members of his family. My mother tells everybody she knows in the village. Anybody on the local bus hears of my plight. I'm added to prayer lists and maybe the prayer chain. The prayer chain is when somebody from the church rings you up. They just say a short sentence. *Pray for Jill* or *Pray for Brian.* You put down your phone and ring the next person on the list and repeat the sentence. It's basically religious Chinese Whispers. Perhaps the last person in the prayer chain gets *Pray for Bill* or *Pray for Ryan.* Perhaps it doesn't matter who you pray for in the end. How can you even construct a prayer around just a name? But that's all there is in these times of Brain Cancer, right? Just prayers. Prayers for anybody. You don't really need the name or the story. Prayers and candles. My father roaming

from church to church lighting those little cheap candles in some sort of ambling desperation.

As the news escapes like a virus, there are also cards. Surprise presents that appear in boxes. Thoughtful messages. Endless flower deliveries. My kitchen looks like there has been a death already. I know many kind people, and I am grateful. I have to tell work that I will not be returning, that I cannot complete my notice period. It is a very attention seeking way to leave a job. They send me a leaving card, but it is also a sorry-you-have-cancer card which makes for some awkward messages.

Brown Eyes and I return to the hospital to meet the neurosurgeons, and to meet our special nurse who is too kind and makes me cry. Before the senior neurosurgeon enters the room, a less experienced one is talking to us. He seems sad and sorry. He can't really look us in the eye. Do I look like his wife? Does he have children too? He says '*The tumour is in your right frontal lobe. Its location means if we tried to remove it, we would paralyse you down one side of your body. It is inoperable and therefore incurable. I'm afraid this diagnosis is fatal. You will die of this cancer eventually. But, we need to take a biopsy of the tumour to grade the cancer. It is possible with treatment, that you could live for some time.*'

And then we drive home to the children. And we are immersed in cliché. The thing that happens to other people has happened to us. We can't believe this is real. Nothing is real. The shock is cold. Cold waves of shock. We keep going for the boys. What do they want for tea? Do they have clean pyjamas? What shall we do today? Do you want a cup of tea? Is time really still ticking on? Can it not stop for us? We need a moment. Just a moment.

I cry later when the boys are in bed. And I think it's strange how a week ago my life might be long, it was reasonable to expect it might be quite long, and now I will only live for *some time*. Which is code for *quite a short time*. Google is not my friend, but I run to her like a moth to a blow-torch and find out what *live for some time* really means. It means at the best, five years. I've gone from a life stretching ahead, to hoping for five years. We bought our younger boy goldfish for his birthday, and you know their life expectancy is 5-10 years. The *fucking goldfish* are going to outlive me! They have years of swimming in circles to look forward to! I would be lucky to have five human years. Five years is endless now, some sort of gift. Please add that to the prayer chain. Say my name and add that all she wants is to live to 45. She wants to outlive the goldfish. Is that too much to ask?

I go back to hospital for two nights. I'm taken to the operating room. There are so many people around me as they get me ready for sleep. There are so many people needed when they have to slice a piece of your brain out. When they drill into your skull and get out a bit of brain. Do I want that bit of brain? I wonder. It might have cancer, but what else does it have? Is it a bit of memory? Is it a bit of something that is inexplicably me? Do I need it? Who will I be when I wake up from this? Will I wake up?

The nurses and doctors around me are kind and brilliant. They talk in their voices from around the world. I am grateful, oh so grateful. I close my eyes in my NHS privilege. I can give my brain to the safety of international expertise. I think of some poor woman in Syria with a brain tumour who doesn't even have a hospital to go to. A woman somewhere in Tanzania who is walking around with a visible tumour, a lump pushing out of her skull. The specialist neuro-anaesthetist from Lithuania is ready to administer the medicine. You know, one of those fucking Europeans who came here and took our jobs. One of those *foreigners* who came here and had the nerve to save our lives with their hard work and years of dedication. And as I drop into the black, I think this is what humanity looks like. The people at my bed are humanity. The NHS is love and humanity.

I wake up in intensive care. And I know this is when I need to dig, I need to dig deep for something. What have I got? I've got jokes. The jokes are still coming. They are sick and tainted and dark, but they always were. And I have my grandmother, my grandmother talking. Something about strength. Something about light and peace. Something about beauty. This is my inner grandmother. And my inner mother. And the women who came before. I've heard their stories. They were spiritualists, they talked to the dead. At some point, tracing back along the lines,

116

they must have been witches. We were burnt, at some point something inside me was definitely burnt. So I'm going to sit up like a rising witch. *I don't need the oxygen mask, thank you very much. Yes, I'm ready to see my husband, thank you. Yes, I will have chocolate and a cup of tea, thank you for everything. And, yes, please move me to the ward, I feel fine.*

I don't know if I feel fine. But it's not relevant, is it? What matters is that I will eat breakfast. That I will apply make-up and put my jewellery back on. I will talk to the woman opposite me. I will offer her comfort. I will clean her table with anti-bacterial wipes because the cleaners are busy. I will talk to the man outside on the balcony who is crying for his dying brain-cancer wife, and I will smile.

Soon I'm at home with a neat row of staples in my head. I'm home to receive biopsy results. The cancer is stage 2-3. Probably more of a 3 than a 2, but we can hope otherwise. I'm lucky it is not 4. It seems odd there are only 4 cancer stages – we need more, we need more stages. The tumour is a rare Astrocytoma – *Astro* to mean star, star-shaped cells. I have stars, actual stars in my brain. I think of the picture they showed us, the mass, the stars, the white spot at the centre, glowing like a demon. I grew that cancer all by myself. And what is cancer? It means crab. When a tumour is surrounded by swollen blood vessels, it looks like the legs of a crab. A crab in my brain. Something moving sideways, pinching, moving in my brain. I grew a crab, a crab whose shell is covered in stars. Was I born with it? Have I had it since my teenage years or my early twenties? Has my whole life been a crab, been a star? Am I nothing but a brain tumour? And if I am, I think that might be OK. Something organic does not feel like an invader or an imposter to me. I love my brain, so I have to love the stars. I hope the mass will change, I hope it will shrink, I hope it will be quiet, but I cannot hope it never existed. There is another story emerging now, another series of things to learn, another life. It is a story that must start with acceptance, because anger and fear have nothing, have nothing for me.

Cancer though, cancer is a big word. There are people on the television telling me to Stand Up To It – and I don't know what this means. What do I do? How do I stand up? There are people telling me in well-meant cards to *fight*. What do I fight? I have only known I have had it for a couple of weeks when people start calling me *brave*. I look up *brave*. It means you are *ready to face or endure danger or pain*. That sounds horrible. I'm not ready for danger or pain. Who is? I have no choice. If I haven't chosen this, I can't possibly be brave. The internet tells me I'm supposed to do something now I have cancer, particularly as mine will never go into remission, will never get better. There are blogs. There are podcasts. If I don't have a blog or podcast, I'm definitely supposed to be doing something extraordinary like training for a triathlon, or at least just raising lots of money for a cancer charity. I'm not even on Instagram, but perhaps now I should join and post pictures of me prematurely shaving my head or the healthy food I'm going to eat now for every meal. Or should I be setting up a fundraising page for myself, asking for money, especially as I'm a mother of two children. The internet has also told me that mothers with cancer are definitely more tragic than women with cancer who don't have children.

I find lots of newspaper articles about cancer mums. Most of them seem to be writing cards for their children to open on their future birthdays when they are dead. I'm not sure about the ghost-cards. I'm not sure I would want a card from a dead person, particularly as I might be enjoying my birthday, not thinking about what I have lost. There are also lists you can make, lists of what you hope for your children. These seem like just another lot of instructions for your partner. Just a way of telling them what to do from the grave. So if I'm not writing cards or lists, then surely I'm supposed to write my own list, a bucket list of what I would like to do before I die. The bucket list are the things you really want to do before you die, before you kick the bucket. Kicking the bucket was what happened to people who were executed by hanging. They definitely didn't get to make a list.

As I think about a list, I realise there is absolutely nothing I want to do, with the exception of finding out what happened to Madeleine McCann, which cannot be easily arranged. I definitely don't want any forced special trips, any organised fun. Why does knowing you have less time mean you must suddenly fill every minute? Why can't I still waste it, like everybody else? Perhaps my bucket list could just be things that deliberately waste time. *Daytime TV. Middle-of-the-day naps. Re-watching favourite films. Re-reading favourite books. A slow walk around the streets where I live.* Maybe then I won't have to be a professional cancer patient.

But I don't judge the cancer people. They have to do what they have to do. And if the blogs and the podcasts and the photographs and the money and the cards and the lists help them, and help others, inspire others, make others not feel alone, then all power to them. I wish them only the best. This is a hard road and you have to do whatever works for you.

In the meantime, we continue to decorate our house, and as our bedroom is next, we are sleeping in the lounge. It is cosy here, but the steroids have built up in my body and they don't want me to sleep. I'm high, and I'm awake all night, listening to the sounds on the street, and letting my manic mind race. I cannot stop composing emails to people, forming drafts that will never be written. I am consumed by death admin at 4am. In these forever-nights, my thoughts are vivid and powerful, and in some strange way I'm feeling liberated. Strangely liberated. I am free of something. The chaos of illness and premature death is allowing me to be myself more intensely and securely. I'm free to feel and behave in ways that normal rules don't allow. There is definitely a Cancer Card and it does not seem all bad to have one in your back pocket.

But as the morning finally comes, I'm thinking about the end, the end of this. I've let myself read the accounts, even watch the videos. Bloated people, people who have lost their sight, their movement, their words, their thoughts. Is that where this leads? Is that what I will be when my brain surrenders to the starry crab? Is that the one-track route I am slithering down, like a slow slide from a mountain, like a freeze-frame car crash? Because I will need to stop the wreckage. I'm relieved for the heroin dealer who lives across the road and cheerfully throws packages out of his window. There must be a way out surely. Are there ways out? Is disintegration inevitable? How much will I have to suffer?

I can suffer. I know about pain. I know about madness, about brain invasion. I'm not sad for me. But I'm sad for my children, sad that I may leave them too soon. All I am is this fierce love, this fierce love that I have poured into them without restraint. I

119

cannot bear to hurt them, to imagine how they might feel if I am no longer here. But life is cruel, it is cruel and it is real. I cannot protect them from everything and that is the reality they may have to learn. I can only trust that if I have to leave them, Brown Eyes will do all the things he needs to. And that these early years of love, such love for them, will count for something, will live somewhere, will remain.

Brown Eyes is calm. He is calm, and wise and loving, and everything you could ever want. I wonder if perhaps he is too calm. I ask him if he has cried. *'Once'* he says, *'When I was in the car alone. A song came on'*

'What was it I ask?' 'The Proclaimers' he says.

'The FUCKING PROCLAIMERS! What song?'

'They only have one song don't they?'

'Why would that make you cry? You don't even like the Proclaimers!'

'I know' he says, *'It was just when they are talking about walking five hundred miles.'*

I'm outraged by his lack of poetry, but you know I should be pleased. He is fine, he is doing fine. He would walk five hundred miles if it would help.

The first few months pass, and I come off the steroids. The thoughts of certain and imminent death calm down a little. Where before I felt that I couldn't really focus on or enjoy anything if I was slowly dying, that urgency fades away. I am looking death firmly in the eye, and I am not denying it, but I'm also trying to survive. Survive as long as possible so I can look after my children, so I can provide them what they need. I am also remembering that nobody actually knows when they are going to die, and I'm not necessarily any further along the road than anybody else.

I have more important things to do now. I have an allergic reaction to an anti-seizure medication that has resulted in a horrific rash. I wait for hours in A&E and eventually see a doctor who wants to repeatedly draw a picture of my body swelling up. *This is what might happen* he wants me to know. I'm admitted to hospital. There is a poor old lady with dementia who is screaming and trying to walk up and down the ward until 3am. Somebody comes to sedate her, and within seconds of the jab in her arm, she is snoring. We are all awake though, all awake and I'm in some kind of stupor on a drip full of anti-histamines. I'm so happy to be sent home.

I am referred to the cancer hospital. I will be treated with six and a half weeks of daily radiation and a low dose of chemotherapy at the same time. For the radiation, I have a mask fitted to cover my face which is then secured to the table during the treatment. It is like a scene from a horror film, or a bit S&M depending on what you are into. I get used to it surprisingly quickly. I don't have many side- effects from the treatment, except the hair falling out from one side of my head. I expected it to shed slowly, groups of hairs at a time, like a cat. But instead it comes out one Saturday in a huge tangled ball. My boys are not alarmed. The eldest puts it gallantly in the bin. I don't really mind as I look pretty good in hats.

The hardest part of the treatment is the constant schlep to the hospital, with Brown Eyes having to drive there every day. Spending so much time at the cancer hospital is not great either. Everybody has cancer for a start. I find myself looped into constant conversations, mainly with older people. Many of them are very fed up with the hospital, very fed up with treatment. They are finding chemotherapy in their 80s difficult. As I'm now hoping I might make it to 45, and 50 is just a distant dream, I find it a bit difficult to be sympathetic to some of the older people. They have had long lives. I wonder if many of them have realised that you do have to die of something at some point. I don't understand why some are even having such intensive treatment. Do they want to live so much? Or are they just afraid to die? I'm not sure I even mind if I don't make my 50s. I wasn't looking forward to the menopause and potentially losing my looks. I wasn't looking forward to my boys moving away and not phoning me anymore. I don't really understand the desire to be a grandparent. And old age does look a little bit rubbish. But I do want to live long enough for my children not to be little. I just want enough time to guide them out of the little years and into the older ones.

But even I am lucky, so lucky. In a separate building, there are children with cancer, teenagers with cancer. Little people who have not yet had a life. Little people suffering the unthinkable, having treatments in brightly painted rooms, while their parents' hearts break slowly, slowly over time like some kind of torture. I cannot imagine their torment, their agonies.

As the treatment continues, cancer becomes normal. Just an everyday existence. Just one thing in my life, in my busy, normal life. The cards and flowers have fallen away, and some people, some friends have fallen too. They didn't know what to say perhaps. They didn't want to think about mortality maybe, or what it might be like to not see your children grow up. There are some who evaporate quickly or don't get in touch at all. Then they are the others, who move in closer. Who tell me they love me. Who are here. Who stay here. They are here if I need something. And what do I need? Just what I always needed. Funny stories. Dark jokes. Long chats about love and sex and relationships and politics and people. Just the good stuff. Life. I need life. It's still running through my veins, and I want to talk about it.

The treatment ends. Another brain scan, with the cannula in your arm, and the dye, and the machine and the headphones over the ear plugs, is done. It shows my tumour has shrunk by a third. A whole third has been burnt away from my brain. What I have lost? Just cancer, just crabs and stars and cells that are sick, sick and wrong? Or have I burnt other cells too? Have some memories been thrown on the fire? Or have I lost some of my mathematics skills when I had very few to start with? Have they torched my total lack of spatial awareness? Could I meet my driving instructor now and behave like a new person? Or are there no benefits to be gained here? Only losses. A bad bit and a good bit of brain in the smoke. A sacrifice I had to make.

I must now start the chemotherapy in monthly cycles at a much higher dose than I have had before. I go to the hospital so they can look at my blood. They worry about platelets, which makes me think of the earth shifting, but it is actually about blood. Blood clotting, blood shifting. And then I go home with the toxic little capsules, a medicine that has an information leaflet that you must never read, unless you want to know you are being poisoned, slowly. And you take them for 5 days. And you are only able to put them in your mouth and swallow them down, because they might save your life. They might be the only thing left that can save you. That can save your brain.

And there are sickness tablets that stop the sickness. And there is a feeling that all food is terrible, and you might just never eat again. And there is retching over the kitchen sink while I cook pizza for the children. And there is no hair loss, which allows me to be disguised. I'm wandering about Sainsbury's on chemotherapy. I'm at the school gate on chemotherapy. I'm at the swimming pool on chemotherapy.

And then the cycle ends. And you wait for the next one.

Another scan tells me my brain tumour is stable. No change. And everyone says *You have never been stable before* and we laugh.

After a year of chemotherapy, I go to the hospital to find out how my tumour has appeared on its latest photograph. Brown Eyes has to work, so I am with my friend L. The doctor is serious as he tells me it has progressed. It has changed. It is a hopeless rebel, an addict who has run from rehab, an athlete who has returned to doping. I go to the café to tell L who is waiting for me. And we cry.

Then I step outside into a bleak November and phone Brown Eyes. When I return, L is being comforted by a woman in a peach dressing gown, attached to an IV pole, who looks just weeks from death. This is how the end is, it seems. Out in public in pastel bed-wear, chained to treatment like a medical prisoner, giving out hugs to strangers, awash with love and peace, or is it pools of fear, flooding out? On the drive home, L and I are crying and laughing, crying and laughing, lost in some sort of absurd hysteria at just how hard it is to exist. As we make our way to pick up our children from the school gate, as we cross the busy road, we imagine we are both hit by a car together, both flung to the ground. We wonder in our last moments, as we clutch our after-school snacks, if we would be relieved. If our last words would be *This shit is over. Goodnight.* But we know this is fiction; we are digging deep in the shadows for jokes, because these will carry us out of this bad-news day. They will forge us further in our friendship, our love for each other.

I find out a week later that I have a place on a clinical trial, to try an experimental drug, alongside a different chemotherapy. How many other patients are on the trial at the hospital? *Only you. You are the first patient on the trial in the UK.* Now I have to be a scientific pioneer. I must drink an experimental liquid drug, 3 times a day that comes in shiny white bottles, fresh from the USA. I must measure it out like methadone, be grateful nobody has tried to flavour it lemon or orange, and I must record in a diary the diarrhoea, and the nausea, and the headaches, and the focal seizures and the dizzy feeling. And I must talk to these little pots of bubbles, these tiny potions, and perhaps make up a spell to chant. Because I'm already on my last life in the cancer game. And everybody knows that is how the treatment works. They cut your cancer, they burn your cancer, they poison your cancer. And when all that has failed, alchemy is next. They mix up something in a cauldron, they hand it over without being able to contain their excitement, and everybody hopes that some kind of wizardry is about to unfold.

On Saturday mornings, I take my boys to football training. One week, we are walking back home, when we stumble into an argument between a football dad and a woman. The woman is outraged that the football dad's son has put a small piece of cling film in her rubbish bin as he walked past. The cling film has been retrieved, but now the dad is furious and throws it on the ground. I pick it up. I tell the dad to do the right thing and put it in his pocket. I tell him not to be angry, to walk away from the woman and her petty argument. To forget about it. He seems grateful. We get home. I re-tell the story to Brown Eyes who is plastering the hallway. My eldest child seems irritated.

'*Mummy*' he says '*Why does every story have to end with you being a hero?*'

I'm annoyed and hurt by this comment. I have to take myself away to another room to calm down. It is here that I realise why I'm annoyed. He might just be right. I thought I was being kind, fuelled by love for strangers, love and kindness that I am trying to teach my children. But do I really mean it? Am I trying to be a fucking hero?

Will this story end with just that? Does just having cancer, having cancer that will certainly kill me, mean I am by default some kind of hero? Was I trying to be that all along? Was all this misadventure and chaos just a reflection of my inner self? Have I been constructing a desperate drama for my whole life, a twisted drama with a tragic finale, like I'm some sort of poor man's Princess Diana?

I need to have a word with myself.
I need to have a word with my mother.
She has something to say about eggs.

Chapter 10

Things I found in the Dark

So I'm thinking. I'm thinking about those words of *heroes or non-heroes*. I'm wondering if my life was a terrible story all along, a film with plot errors, a self-made masterpiece of attention. My childhood was punctuated with *Only You. Only You* would trip on the hoop and be in the landing place of the firework. *Only You* would be bitten by the dog, would fall down the stairs, would hallucinate from the milk. *Only You* would cry at the parties, would not eat the packed lunch. *Only You* would say they saw the angel, and touch the worm. *Only You* would start their period on Christmas Day.

And then the voice moved to the others, the others outside, and they were still saying it. *Only You* would risk this, risk this night. *Only You* would dance on that table. *Only You* would take this too far.

Only You would get this illness, this rare swelling of your body. *Only You* would walk off the plane. *Only You* would match the paedophiles, would release the Anthrax. *Only You* and the Floozy T-shirt, the Ricin, the desk snapped in two. *Only You* and the coach, the empty coach, the brain-man coach. *Only You* and the model, the escort, the rock star, the millionaire. *Only You* and the chance meeting of a gate-crasher. *Only You* and the immediately-ill new love. *Only You* and the car crash, the lost ring, the lost best man. *Only You* and the boss under his desk. *Only You* and the baby born in the bathroom. *Only You* and the baby saved from the floor. *Only You* and the never-seen before allergy to your own baby. *Only You* and the rare knee growth that needs to be photographed and sliced. *Only You* and the dead baby, evaporating with your grandmother.

Only You and the one-in-a million-terminal-star in your brain. That will kill you. That will kill you.

They are still saying it. When I told them, the ones I love about my brain, about the cancer, they all said *Only You*. *This would only happen to you. Of all the people I know, this would happen to you.*

I can even hear *Only You*. Their words meant something else, but maybe I heard it differently on my mother's kitchen radio that would scream when you tuned in the charts. I can hear Alison Moyet. I'm four years old, and my mother is singing again, her beautiful voice singing.

Only You wasn't always said in blame. *Only You* has been said mostly in affection, endearment. But at some point, I have started to wear it like a badge, haven't I? I started living it. I started thinking I was different, that the unthinkable, the storyline you wouldn't bother making up, was constantly rising on the horizon. Maybe I started to enjoy it. Maybe it became self-fulfilling. Maybe it is all my fault. Maybe I made everything happen. We all choose what we say to ourselves about what happened, about how to frame things, about how to tell the story. Maybe I wanted every story to end with me being a hero.

And then my mother, yes my mother.

She is talking about eggs. She is wondering if biology is to blame. She was too old when she had me and her egg was past its sell by date. My raw genetic material was flawed from the get-go. Something is missing, and nobody will ever really know what that is. I can't really take my mother seriously, and she doesn't expect me to. This is a woman who once said about Channel 4+1 '*I don't understand this channel, it seems to be everything that has just already been on Channel 4*'. This is also a woman who is still trying to remember the name of a film she saw in the late 1990s. She went to see it in Tamworth with my father, no specific date is known, not even a year. They cannot remember anything about the plot of the film, or where it was set. They also cannot remember anybody and I mean ANYBODY who was in it. Yet for the last twenty years, my mother will now and again mention the film. '*I wish we could remember what it was*' she will say, '*I wish we could remember. It was a good film.*'

'*But there is nothing to remember* 'I say, '*because you have forgotten everything, can't you see that? You don't have a date, a plot, a name or anybody in it. It has gone. It cannot be remembered.'*

'I don't know' she says. *'I know it was raining when we left the cinema.'*

But maybe my mother is right about the egg. We are all just animals after all. Just the fittest surviving, and the dud eggs, the black sheep, the lame ones, the runts – they are cast aside. They are all destined for biological failure, for premature death. It's just science. If somebody could have written a code for me, some sort of medical code as soon as I was born, maybe that would have helped. Perhaps just eight digits, and perhaps a capital letter and a symbol, and that code could have told us the future. Perhaps I wasn't meant to live long. I was always a stray cat, falling through eight lives with needless oblivion, until it finally slid under a car. Nine chances blown. Nine silly stories. Then dead.

And science. Well only science can save me now. Only the long-researched treatments, the expert judgements of people much cleverer than me, who studied for exams while I was out getting wasted, only they, and their brilliance, can save me. And maybe they will. Maybe *Only You* will live for an unprecedented length of time with this condition. *Only You* will beat the odds. *Only You* will be on a chat show in a decade, a chat show not yet invented, talking about your own survival like a miracle. Ending the story as a hero, again, a different kind of hero.

Or maybe there is another kind of fate. At the religious charity I used to work for, they were at the very top level of pre-destiny. God has a plan for every one of us. They believed we are just living out the plan of the interventionist man. Everything meant something.   And then there is a different God, a God my grandmother and mother talked of. A God who gives us free will. A belief that you have a spirit, you have a soul, and it is going, it is going somewhere. Sometimes something else turns up, turns up in the mix. I know well their stories, and they are my stories. The clocks that stop when somebody dies. The ghosts they can see. The ghosts their ancestors could talk to. Did they carry messages? Did the dead ever have anything to say? Or was it always *Don't forget to pay your gas bill Dot* or, *Stan, the keys you lost are under the doormat.* It seems a shame that this is all that ever comes through from the other side. Surely a Medium should ask first, '*What happens! What happens after death?'* *Tell us everything.* But no, it seems the dead are weighed down, heavy with trivia, living eternally in a sea of small matters.

I grew up in this sense of magic, this sense of spirit – sometimes religious, but mostly just other worldly. We were surrounded by bleak landscapes that spoke this kind of language, the stubby fields, the farmland, our forest. There were many days where we walked around graveyards, reading aloud the names of the dead, or if it was the village graveyard, looking for someone we knew. Dusky winter days, bones underfoot, stories of life and possibly God. The birds that seemed to talk to us. That whole summer we spent on some craggy coastline, calling out for ravens, my father was desperate for ravens. Yet the birds were just black spots in the distance, and he was too. He was always ahead, balancing on the rocks, hands in a state of nature-emergency that we couldn't catch up with. I caught up with him once. It was in France, we saw a Swallowtail, the Queen of Butterflies together. We spotted her together. We couldn't scoop her into the net, but we shared her for a moment. My brother scoured the skies for UFOs. My mother read books about serial killers.

And then I left the countryside for the cities, the cities where the signs of fate are harder to look for. Where do you look? The park is too tame. Maybe you only have the eyes of strangers. Maybe you only have chance encounters on buses which was where my grandmother found her ministry. Or maybe you should look for words painted on walls? Or on mattresses? The abandoned mattresses of South London, they live on every street. They once offered sleep but now they are stained and soaked and unloved. A trip to the dump was too much for their owner. But somebody is painting sayings on them, words of love and peace. I should be taking pictures of the mattresses with sayings, maybe there is a whole story I should be following.

So maybe fate can save me. Maybe the story was written from the beginning. Whether it was the pre-destiny of biology or the plan of some kind of God, maybe the ending was decided before the beginning even started. It was planned inside an egg. It was planned inside a brightly lit meeting room in heaven. It was planned by a congress of ravens, ravens who were hiding from us while they met inside a gap in the rocks.

It is this inner-destiny, this witch that I talk to the most. She brings me comfort with her stories about the colours of souls, she brings me power with the idea I may have senses I haven't yet used. I may have lived lives I have now forgotten. I can dig her up, I can dig her up, and I do. On the scanning table, I pray not for hope, not even for life, just for magic, just for the magic of fate, the order of things. Send me something, some kind of answer. Or did I use up all of the tokens, did I use up all the tokens on Brown Eyes, Brown Eyes and these babies? Because my goodness, they are miracles, they are every-day miracles.

If my inner psychologist is arguing for the self-fulfilled prophecy of my personality, and my inner witch is whispering something about the age of souls, while my bad egg genes continue to rot, I need to listen very carefully. Because there is another voice. Actually it's not a voice; it's a bass drum, it's a whistle at an old-school rave, it's the sound of two cars colliding, it's the cries of an orgasm, it's the cries of the dying, it's the first cry of a baby entering the world, it's every word that's ever been spoken.

It's the sound of chaos.

Chaos is saying that nothing has any meaning at all. There are no plans, no fate, no God, no other worlds. We are just dots, spinning on a planet, in an infinite universe. Everything is random. Nothing matters. Nothing matters at all.

I used to find chaos difficult. I like something impulsive, something wild, but I also like order. I used to try to hold chaos back by touching things in sets of threes. I used to try to tidy away chaos. I found sanctuary in order. But I know order is a big liar; I know she tells me things I don't really need to hear. I know sometimes she stops me living. I know she feasts on fear.

Order tells us that if we do the right things, if we say the right things, if we are the right kind of person, good things will happen. And even if good things don't happen, bad things will stay away. Bad things are not meant for us. Like the plane we ask

130

to stay in the sky, we talk to the future of our fears. We promise it everything. We trust it has a plan that has goodness at its heart.

But it doesn't work. The bad things happen. They happen. They happen anyway. They tell us there wasn't a plan, nobody had a plan for us.

But now, as I look at death in the eye, as we must all do, as we must all surely do, I have something to learn from the chaos.

I already have the things I found in the dark. The songs I sang in my childhood bed, to break the gloom. The teenage wild, lit-up nights that never leave your veins. The things I promised myself about pain in a black hospital dusk. The all-night pharmacies of New York that kept me alive until morning. The boy that appeared in the shade of the party, the only boy, my boy with the beautiful body, with his pockets full of truth and power, his hands like a tourniquet, that stems the bleed, that always stems the bleed. And his babies, the babies that turn your heart over, that turn it right over, and make you wonder if you might bleed again, this time just bleeding out all the love in the world. Just all the love in the world. And then you get right to the bottom of the dark, which is where you find the jokes. These are the jokes that were born of the dark. Something funny is always funny. It cannot stop being funny. These are the jokes that will save you.

But now this is pitch-black dark, these are the really dark times, maybe the end times, and I must step inside into the chaos. The place where life was only ever a series of random events. Where all the control you thought you had was just noise. In this place, nothing matters, nothing can really matter. In this place, there is no order.

Let's have a look inside.

What can you see? Don't you think it is surprisingly light in here? There is definitely a window somewhere. There is music playing, it is very quiet, but your song is playing somewhere in another room. What is your song? You better choose carefully. And there is a mirror on the wall. Go and have a look at yourself. Who are you? You are lots of things people told you that you were, and you are some things you told yourself. You can get rid of any of these things right now if you want to. You can act a different part. Say your name out loud. What does it even mean? It's just a name. Try out a different name if you want to. You are just a dot like anybody else, after all. Just a little bit of dust. That's the good bit. The good bit is that you are dust. In the chaos, you are dust. And then remind yourself, remind yourself now, that the worst has already happened. You are in the really dark times, remember? This is chaos. Take a seat. Feel the cold air of insignificance on your face. Breathe in the value of nothing. Then see what remains. What remains for you? What is left now? What matters?

I think you know what remains. I think you can see what matters.

And so maybe I'll live for a long time.
Or maybe I won't.

And maybe, when the time comes, when the time comes to die, maybe it will be like the film. The late 1990s film that my parents watched in Tamworth. After the viewing, after the story has ended, nobody can really remember the story or where it was set. Who was it about? What was the story anyway? Was the acting any good? Once they have forgotten, it cannot be remembered. The details are dust. It doesn't matter what you do, it's all gone. It's all gone.

But they did remember how they felt when they left the cinema, when the show was over. They remembered that they enjoyed the film, that it left them with something inexplicably happy. So happy they are still trying to recreate it twenty years later.

And then it started to rain. They remember that.

The rain that washes the fields and the streets, the rain that darkens the skies. The rain that cleanses and soothes, and says to the earth, '*Are you ready?* '

And the earth by plan, by chaos always says '*Yes.* '

And the water drenches the land. And the birds scatter from the fields. And new life begins in the soil, in the matter, in the roots.

And in those roots, is the love of the people, the people who loved. Their stories on the earth, written in dust and soil and seeds. Not big stories. Just little stories. About the things they did, the little things they did with love.

And I loved. I loved fiercely like a firework.
Love remains. Love remains.

Love is all there is in the dark.

Printed in Great Britain
by Amazon